GOSPEL CENTRED

PREACHING

Becoming the preacher God wants you to be

by Tim Chester

and Marcus Honeysett

Gospel centred preaching

The Good Book Company
Blenheim House, 1 Blenheim Road, Epsom, Surrey KT19 9AP, UK
Tel: 0333 123 0880; **International**: +44 (0) 208 942 0880
Email: info@thegoodbook.co.uk

Websites:
UK: www.thegoodbook.co.uk
North America: www.thegoodbook.com
Australia: www.thegoodbook.com.au
New Zealand: www.thegoodbook.co.nz

ISBN: 9781909559202

Cover design: André Parker
Printed in China

CONTENTS

Introduction 5
The Principles 8
Finding your way around 10

Part One: The Goals of Preaching
1. Capturing the affections for Christ 13
2. So that lives are changed 19
3. So that God is glorified 25

Part Two: The Means of Preaching
4. The word of God 35
5. The Spirit of God 45
6. The preacher 53

Part Three: The Content of Preaching
7. Preaching good news 61
8. Preaching Christ 67
9. Preaching to unbelievers 77

Part Four: The Priorities of Preaching
10. Make it clear 87
11. Make it real 93
12. Make it felt 101

Part Five: The Process of Preaching
13. Structuring a sermon 111
14. Writing a sermon 119
15. Delivering a sermon 131
16. Preparing a Bible study 141
17. Leading a Bible study 149

Further Reading 155

INTRODUCTION

To preach is a tremendous privilege. It is a beautiful thing to do. Words have power. Even human words can heal and hurt, create and destroy. How much more the words of God.

God created the world by a word. He rules human history through his word. In the Old Testament, whenever the king and the prophet went head to head there was only ever one winner. And now Christ extends his reign through the gospel word. His kingdom grows as we proclaim his word, calling people to the obedience of faith. God's word brings life and freedom. Preaching is to proclaim this life-giving, liberating message of the kingdom of God. Gospel-centred preaching is preaching the gospel to win people's affections for Christ, creating lives that glorify God.

And preaching is fundamentally *the proclamation of good news.* That's what the New Testament words for "preaching" mean: to proclaim, herald or announce. We are messengers from God sent to announce the good news that his King is coming to restore his reign over the earth.

That message, though, is *not* good news to those who are rebels—including you and me. But the good news is that in his grace God offers forgiveness and righteousness through the death and resurrection of his Son. So "everyone who calls on the name of the Lord will be saved" (Romans 10 v 13).

> How, then, can they call on the one they have not believed in? And how can they believe in the one of whom they have not heard? And how can they hear without someone preaching to them? And how can

> anyone preach unless they are sent? As it is written, "How beautiful are the feet of those who bring good news!" **Romans 10 v 14-15**

In one sense *every* Christian is a bearer of the good news. We preach the gospel to ourselves when we resist temptation by reminding ourselves that God is bigger and better than anything sin offers. We preach the gospel to other Christians when we comfort or challenge them with the truth. We preach the gospel to unbelievers when we urge them to follow Christ.

God, however, has also gifted people in the church to preach in more formal contexts—Sunday sermons, interactive Bible studies, children's talks and so on. Our focus in this book is on these more formal times of preaching, especially sermons. We want the word of God to be proclaimed everywhere and all through the week, not just at a formal gathering on Sunday. But public preaching shapes the culture of a church and sets the agenda for life-on-life discipleship.

How to use this book

This workbook is designed so you can read it on your own or as part of a group, with questions for personal reflection or group discussion.

It can also form the curriculum for preaching training for a small or larger group. You could cover a chapter at each meeting of the group, along with other exercises. Or it could be studied more intensively with one part per session (perhaps with people choosing between chapters 13-15 and 16-17, depending on the ministry in which they're involved).

Alternatively, you could work through this book one to one with a partner as you encourage each other to grow as preachers.

Here are some regular training exercises you could do alongside the material in this book:

1. **Preaching preparation:** Working on a passage together from scratch to model how to handle the Bible and shape your work into a sermon.

2. **Preaching workshop:** Asking participants to preach a short message before receiving peer feedback.
3. **Preaching debrief:** Discussing sermons with a more experienced preacher to explore together how you arrived at your understanding of the passage, and then shaped it into a sermon.

A word of warning

God says:

> These are the ones I look on with favour: those who are humble and contrite in spirit, and who trembles at my word.” **Isaiah 66 v 2**

We need to listen to sermons with discernment, subjecting them to the ultimate authority of God’s word. But the greater danger for most of us is that of learning to listen to sermons with a critical spirit. We evaluate the preacher rather than allowing ourselves to be evaluated by God’s word. This workbook will encourage us to think about what sermons should accomplish and how they do that. But the more you think about the mechanics of a sermon, the greater the danger of this kind of punditry. We need to be people who tremble at God’s word however it is being preached.

A word of acknowledgement

Many people have influenced our preaching, some by talking about it and many more by modelling it. More than any other source, Tim learned to preach by listening to his father, Richard Chester. Not only did he provide a fine model of preaching, he also laid the theological foundations of Tim’s life. Richard allowed us to plunder his notes on training preachers for this book.

Marcus looks back with gratitude to church and mission leaders who, when he was in his late teens and early 20s, encouraged him to have a go and were incredibly gracious with his stumbling first steps. There is nothing better for junior preachers than having encouraging, wise role models.

The Principles

The Goals of Preaching

1. **Capturing the affections for Christ:** The goal of preaching is *to capture the affections of our hearts for Christ.*

2. **So that lives are changed:** The goal of preaching is to capture the affections of our hearts for Christ *so that lives are changed.*

3. **So that God is glorified:** The goal of preaching is to capture the affections of our hearts for Christ so that lives are changed *so that God is glorified.*

The Means of Preaching

4. **The word:** Effective preachers trust in the authority of the Bible.

5. **The Spirit:** Effective preachers trust in the power of the Spirit.

6. **The preacher:** Effective preachers trust in the character of God.

The Content of Preaching

7. **Preaching good news:** Because the gospel is good news, your sermon should be good news.

8. **Preaching Christ:** Because the whole Bible points to Christ, your sermon should point to Christ.

9. Preaching to unbelievers: Because our problem is the heart, your sermon should address the heart.

The Priorities of Preaching

10. Make it clear: Your sermon should make the passage clear.

11. Make it real: Your sermon should make the passage real.

12. Make it felt: Your sermon should make the passage felt.

The Process of Preaching

13. Structuring a sermon: Ensure everything contributes to your main aim.

14. Writing a sermon: Let the word do the work.

15. Delivering a sermon: Passionate preaching requires a passionate preacher.

16. Preparing a Bible study: Help people discover the message of the text by asking good questions.

17. Leading a Bible study: Keep people focused on the message of the text and its implications.

Finding your way around

Consider this

A scenario—often based on a real-life situation—which raises some kind of dilemma or frustration in gospel ministry.

Bible background

A relevant Bible passage together with some questions to help you think it through.

Read all about it

A discussion of the principle, both in terms of its theological underpinning and its contemporary application.

Questions for reflection

Questions that can be used for group discussion or personal reflection.

Ideas for action

Some ideas or an exercise to help people think through the application of the principle to their own situation.

We have tried to make this book work:

- whether it is read by an individual or used as the basis for group discussion.
- whether you want to work through it systematically or turn to particular topics as they arise in church life.

PART ONE

THE GOALS OF PREACHING

1 CAPTURING THE AFFECTIONS FOR CHRIST

Principle

The goal of preaching is to *capture the affections of our hearts for Christ.*

Consider this

I, Marcus, was speaking at a meeting of Christian students. The young man leading the meeting invited me to come to the front while he prayed for me. "We're delighted to have a guest speaker tonight who's going to come to teach us the Bible." "Hmm," I thought. "True, but not true."

He prayed and I was left in front of the microphone. "Actually I'm not just going to teach the Bible," I began. "I'm going to preach the gospel." As I looked out at the group I could see a number of them thinking: "What's the difference?"

Bible background

Read 2 Corinthians 4 v 1-6

- What should preachers not do?

- What exactly *is* preaching according to these verses?

- What is the goal of preaching?

Read all about it

Gospel preaching must involve teaching the Bible. Our authority comes from God's word and that word must be understood. That's the purpose of explanation. Anything less than this and our preaching will lack substance and rely on human power.

But preaching is so much more than simply teaching the Bible. Vaughan Roberts, President of The Proclamation Trust in the UK, says: "I always feel a little uncomfortable when I'm about to speak and someone says, 'Vaughan's just about to teach the Bible to us'." He explains: "That's *part* of what I'm doing, but I shouldn't just be teaching the Scriptures so people understand them. I should be longing and praying and preaching, as far as I'm able, that people will be so captivated and amazed by this truth that their hearts will be filled with love for God and amazement at his glory." [1]

Preaching is:

- **Proclaiming** God's word in such as way that people see God's greatness and rejoice in his total supremacy.
- **Presenting** the *light* of God so that, through the Holy Spirit, people might get taken up with the *person* of God.
- **Speaking** the words of God to extend the reign of God in people's hearts, so that they yearn with David: "as the deer pants for streams of water so my soul pants for you" (Psalm 42 v 1).
- **Proclaiming** good news of peace with God so that rebels submit to him and enjoy him for ever.
- **Presenting** the surpassing treasure of God so that people love him more than life.
- **Leading** people in the ways of God so that—taught, corrected, reproved and trained in righteousness—we might be equipped for every good work.

1 Vaughan Roberts, "An Exposition of 1 Peter 1 v 1-12," Proclamation Trust Younger Ministers Conference 2013, www.proctrust.org.uk/dls/YMC2013-01-01.mp3.

These are all different facets of the same truth: preaching is so much more than simply a process of education. It is capturing affections for Christ. We can do no better than the definition of the Puritan Cotton Mather. He said the aim of preaching was "to restore the throne and dominion of God in the hearts of men." [1]

Affections and emotions

By affections we do not simply mean *emotions*. It's great when someone has an emotional response to a sermon. But it's not a good measure of God's work. A comedian can make people laugh and a good story-teller can make them cry. We're after more than laughter and tears. Our affections are the motives that drive our behaviour and emotions—our desires, convictions, hopes, fears and longings. The Bible summarises this with its focus on the heart.

The heart in the Bible represents our desires and beliefs. Proverbs 4 v 23 says: "Above all else, guard your heart, for it is the wellspring of life" (ESV). In other words, our behaviour and emotions flow out of our hearts. Jesus, too, says behaviour comes "from within, out of a person's heart" (Mark 7 v 20-23). So if we want our preaching truly to change behaviour then we need to ensure it first changes hearts. Behaviour follows belief. Otherwise we're just manipulating people and that's legalism. "Above all else, guard your heart, for it is the wellspring of life" is not just key to living. It's also key to gospel-centred preaching.

So preaching is about capturing the affections of our heart for Christ so that our confidence is in Christ, and our longing is to know him and to see him glorified. Jesus said: "The kingdom of heaven is like treasure hidden in a field. When a man found it, he hid it again, and then in his joy went and sold all he had and bought that field." (Matthew 13 v 44). The job of the preacher is to point the way to this treasure so that people give all they have to take hold of it. And that's not all. Our job is to point to the treasure that is ours in Christ so that people, like the man in the parable, do this *with joy*.

1 Quoted in John Piper, *The Supremacy of God in Preaching*, Baker, 2nd Ed., 2004, p25.

What is preaching for?

In 2 Corinthians 4 v 5-6 Paul says: "For what we preach is not ourselves, but Jesus Christ as Lord, and ourselves as your servants for Jesus' sake. For God, who said, 'Let light shine out of darkness,' made his light shine in our hearts to give us the light of the knowledge God's glory displayed in the face of Christ." *What is the goal of preaching?* It is that the light of God might shine in people's hearts. It is that people might see the light of the glory of God in the face of Christ.

Consider the New Testament word "exhortation". It implies so much more than the acquisition of more information. Or consider the word "heed". To heed God's word is not only to know it. Preaching is not simply a process of education. It's a process of change.

And this is not just a matter of definitions. It makes a huge difference to how you approach preparing and delivering sermons or Bible talks. It means that when you reach the point where you're confident you've understood the passage, you're actually only halfway through your preparation. **It means that if all you've done is explain the passage, then you haven't done your job.**

Working on the text and giving a message are not the same task. Of course they *are* closely related because doing good work in the text is the essential starting point to delivering a powerful biblical message. Good preaching is *never anything less* than Bible teaching. As Paul says, "We do not preach ourselves." We're not presenting human wisdom or depending on human eloquence. A few verses earlier he says: "We have renounced secret and shameful ways; we do not use deception, nor do we distort the word of God. On the contrary, by setting forth the truth plainly we commend ourselves to everyone's conscience in the sight of God." (2 Corinthians 4 v 2). Good preaching always involves presenting the word of God plainly. The message and its applications have to be rooted in the text and flow from the text.

But good preaching is always *more than teaching*. We're not just giving expository lectures. Working on the text and preaching a sermon have different goals. The aim of text work is understanding truth. What is God saying? Why is he saying it? How is he saying it? What is his purpose? These are all important questions. But the aim of a sermon is to take us beyond simply understanding a text to adoration, thanksgiving, obedience and joy. Merely to know the truth is the position of the demons (James 2 v 19).

The key is to ask this question: what is the biblical author trying to *achieve* through this passage? And *how* is he trying to get the response he wants? This is different to asking *what* he is saying. The application of the passage (rather than comprehension of its content) is the *point* of the passage – and therefore the point of preaching the passage.

Most sermons mostly contain ideas that most of the congregation already know. So if you think of preaching primarily as communicating ideas, then most sermons are just a waste of time. Or you will see the preacher's job as being to unearth some fresh insight—however obscure or eccentric. You will go after novelty.

The main exception to most ideas already being known by the congregation is evangelistic sermons. But here it's even more important to capture the affections because unbelievers are not predisposed to accept what's being said. We need to make them want to believe so they're willing to give the time to engage with whether it really is true. With both believers and unbelievers the aim of preaching is for the word of God to capture people's hearts.

Ideas for action

Step One: Pursue God in his word until he moves your heart

When preparing, work on the text until it moves you. Begin by praying that the Holy Spirit would capture your affections through the word. It might be that the passage excites you or disturbs you or challenges you or comforts you. It might move you to adore Christ or fear God or confess your sin or speak of Christ boldly or obey its commands. You might laugh, you might cry, you might tremble, you might shout for joy. But pursue God in his word until it moves you.

Step Two: Make your aim to move the hearts of your hearers in the same way

Take whatever it is in the text that moves your heart and present that to the congregation so their hearts are moved in a similar way. Not only will you be directing the passage to people's hearts, you'll also preach with the passion and conviction that come from the word having first impacted your heart. Of course, realistically you won't move all the people all the time! But unless you aim to capture people's affections for Christ, you'll probably end up moving none of the people none of the time.

Questions for reflection

John Stott describes five "paradoxes" of Christian preaching. He says it is:

1. Both **biblical** and **contemporary** (relating the ancient text to the modern context).
2. Both **authoritative** and **tentative** (distinguishing between the infallible word and its fallible interpreters).
3. Both **prophetic** and **pastoral** (combining faithfulness with gentleness).
4. Both **gifted** and **studied** (necessitating a divine gift and human self-discipline).
5. Both **thoughtful** and **passionate** (letting the heart burn as Christ opens to us the scriptures).[1]

? For each of these paradoxes, on which side are you strongest or weakest?

1 John Stott, *The Living Church*, IVP, 2007, p116.

2 SO THAT LIVES ARE CHANGED

Principle

The goal of preaching is to capture the affections of our hearts for Christ *so that lives are changed.*

Consider this

No-one could deny that Colin knew his Bible. He quoted it liberally in his public prayers. He was always pointing to obscure cross-references in Bible studies. He often corrected Phil's preaching. What's more, he was usually right. So why, thought Phil to himself, was he such a pain? Why was he so slow to serve?

Part of the problem was that Colin thought of himself as a mature Christian. After all, no-one in the church knew their Bible as well as Colin. So what was going wrong?

Bible background

Read James 1 v 19-27

- What is the aim of preaching the word?
- How do you evaluate good preaching?
- How does James evaluate good preaching?
- How does James define good listening?
- What does gospel religion look like?

Read all about it

James 1 v 22 says: "Do not merely listen to the word, and so deceive yourselves. Do what it says."

That surely is a statement of the obvious. Hearing God's word is neither here nor there. Merely knowing the truth is of no value. As James goes on to say: "Faith by itself, if it is not accompanied by action, is dead ... You believe that there is one God. Good! Even the demons believe that—and shudder" (James 2 v 17, 19). *What counts is what we do with what we hear.*

So growing in Christian maturity is not about receiving and mentally acknowledging the correctness of Bible teaching, as if in a lecture. Maturity is about living out the call of Christ to be disciples and make disciples. You can consume all the church sermons you like and be just as immature at the end as at the beginning if all you do is passively listen. Indeed, Jesus seems to suggest that not putting into practice what we hear is actually worse than not hearing it (Luke 10 v 8-12).

"Do not merely listen to the word, and so deceive yourselves. Do what it says." This statement is clearly true. Yet James still feels the need to state it. This statement has radical implications for our preaching. It means the measure of good preaching is *not what people hear*, but *what people do* as a result. It means that what counts is not so much good Bible *teaching* as good Bible *living*. Of course, good Bible living requires good Bible teaching. But Bible teaching is not an end in itself. You can have a church with good Bible teaching that is not a Bible church.

Here's an experiment we *don't* suggest you try at home. Take a baby and put it in its high chair. Then for a month each meal time present it with steaks, vegetables and fruit. What's going to happen? The point is this: **it's not the quality or quantity of food you put before babies that makes them grow—it's the amount they digest.** It's the same with Christians. It's not the quality or quantity of Bible teaching you put before them that makes them grow. It's the amount they digest.

Think about it now. If the measure of a good sermon is changed lives, how might that change your approach? If the goal of your church is not good Bible teaching *per se*, but good Bible living, how might that change your approach?

1. Preaching to create disciples

One implication is that the goal of our preaching should be changed lives. Our aim is to create disciples who deny themselves, take up their cross and follow Jesus (Mark 8 v 34).

It is wonderfully true that Bible teaching builds up a repository of gospel knowledge that provides people with a solid foundation for their lives. More often than I can count, I've had reason to reflect that people who are well taught cope better with adversity than those who have to learn truth in the moment. A crisis, for example, is a bad time to teach people the sovereignty of God. But people who understand God's sovereign care and loving discipline tend to respond better to tragedy. Prevention is better than cure.

Yet it's also possible to know all about God's sovereignty and still go to pieces in a crisis. The truth needs to be connected to daily life. And that's a job for both the speaker and the listener.

Preaching is not simply about providing some information that may be useful at some later point. Preaching is about effecting change in the moment as the Holy Spirit applies what is being said to people's hearts. Our goal should be a change of heart in and through the sermon that leads to a change of life.

You grow in maturity by *living* the gospel. And that requires opportunities to live for Jesus as well as opportunities to hear the Bible preached. Consider how Jesus trained his disciples. He got them to accompany him, he sent them out to do ministry for themselves, he asked them questions, he answered questions, and he reflected with them on events.

People can delude themselves into thinking they're growing in maturity simply because they're growing in knowledge. Our western education environment with its emphasis on academic attainment makes us particularly susceptible to this mistake. It is easy to think of a sermon in terms of a lesson or lecture. The measure of maturity becomes attending services or knowing facts about the Bible instead of loving Christ, trusting his word and serving him in the world.

2. Preaching to create disciple-makers

Sermons are a vital part of the work of any biblical church. But preaching is more than Sunday sermons. Preaching is the proclamation of the gospel. As Phillip D. Jensen and Paul Grimmond remind us, "sermons and preaching are not synonymous. Biblical preaching is about communicating God's thoughts and not our own. And so we preach biblically whenever and wherever we declare the word of God to each other. In fact, sometimes there may even be more preaching happening over morning tea than from the pulpit, if dozens of conversations revolve around sharing God's word of encouragement and rebuke with one another. Sermons, in other words, are a subset of a larger activity—the activity of proclaiming God's word to one another, and from one generation to the next. Preaching is an activity that all are called on to perform." [1]

The word of God is far too important to the life of individual Christians, and the life of the church and its mission to be confined to 30 minutes on a Sunday morning. The word needs to permeate all areas of church life. We need preaching on Monday mornings as well as Sunday mornings.

- We need to preach the gospel to our own hearts to counter temptation.
- We need to preach the gospel to other Christians in everyday conversation by exhorting one another to follow Christ.
- We need to preach the gospel to unbelievers by pointing them to Christ.

This preaching might not have three points and it's unlikely to last for 30 minutes at a time! But it's a vital proclamation of the gospel.

1 Phillip D. Jensen and Paul Grimmond, *The Archer and the Arrow: Preaching the very words of God*, Matthias Media, 2010, p14-15.

So one of the aims of our sermons should be to equip people so they themselves can preach the truth to others, so they can be disciple-makers. In your sermons include suggestions of how and when people might speak the truth in love to one another. Be intentional about presenting a good model for handling the Bible and applying the Bible.

People often ask me (Tim) about the discipleship programme in our churches. I think they're asking about what courses we run. I wonder how Jesus or Paul might have answered that question. For them discipleship involved living and working together. The gospel was applied to people's lives in the course of everyday life. So in our church we encourage people to see the weekly sermon as our discipleship programme. This is what then sets the agenda for one-to-one discipleship through the week. The Sunday sermon gives a natural platform to apply God's word to specific issues in people's lives.

Questions for reflection

- Evaluate a recent sermon. What life change did it commend? What gospel motives for change did it give?

- Evaluate the preaching of your church. Are lives being changed? How can you know? How are people being encouraged to engage with God's word for themselves? Are people discipled at a personal level? What opportunities are there for people to serve Christ? Are they encouraged to see all of life as a context for service?

- How are you preaching the gospel on Monday morning—to yourself and others?

3 SO THAT GOD IS GLORIFIED

Principle

The goal of preaching is to capture the affections of our hearts for Christ so that lives are changed *so that God is glorified.*

Consider this

John Piper tells how one Sunday he preached on the holiness of God from Isaiah 6, trying as best he could "to display the majesty and glory of such a great and holy God". What he didn't know was that in the congregation was a young family who had just discovered that their child had been sexually abused by a close relative.

If you'd known that news, what theme would you have taken?

Later the father told Piper: "John, these have been the hardest months of our lives. Do you know what has gotten me through? The vision of the greatness of God's holiness that you gave me the first week of January. It has been the rock we could stand on."[1]

Why do you think he said this?

1 John Piper, *The Supremacy of God in Preaching*, Baker, 2004, p13-14.

Bible background

Read Ephesians 1 v 3-17

- What is the goal of God's work in our lives?
- What is the link between Paul's description of God's work in our lives in verses 3-14 and his prayer in verse 17?
- What are the implications of these verses for our preaching?

Read all about it

Ephesians 1 v 3-14 is one long, single sentence in which Paul expounds the work of salvation. Three times he says God has blessed us in Christ "to the praise of his glorious grace" or "for the praise of his glory" (6, 12, 14). Each of these phrases is the climax of a section focusing on the work of each member of the triune God.

The praise of God's glory

The Father has chosen us for adoption *to the praise of his glorious grace*. The Son has redeemed and will become head of all *to the praise of his glory*. The Spirit has sealed us as the promise of a coming inheritance *to the praise of his glory*. Father, Son and Spirit pursue the praise of each other. The Father delights to see his Son glorified. The Son delights to see his Father praised. The Spirit delights to see the Father revealed in the Son. All that God does aims at his glory. All that he does in us is done that he might be glorified in us.

Paul then says: "I keep asking that the God of our Lord Jesus Christ, the glorious Father, may give you the Spirit of wisdom and revelation, so that you may know him better" (v 17). Paul tells the Ephesians what God has done in Christ. Then he prays that the Spirit might enlighten them so they *comprehend* what God has done in Christ. And all for the praise of his glorious grace. Our lives are for the magnification of the greatness of the glory of God's grace.

So the main aim of our preaching should be that people magnify the greatness of the glory of the grace of God in Christ. If that is God's purpose for creation and his purpose for our lives and his purpose for his church, then it ought to be the purpose of everything we do in a local church—including preaching. Indeed, the aim of preaching should be constantly to realign our lives and our life together to the glory of God. We are always getting distracted by the glory of other things or by our own self-glory. Preaching should present God afresh so that anew, and in increasing measure, our preoccupation is with God's glory. Like Paul in Ephesians 1, we should proclaim what God has done for us in Christ, and pray for "the Spirit of wisdom and revelation" to reveal God through our proclamation so that people praise his glorious grace.

So the goal of our preaching is the glory of God. God is glorified when hearts are set on fire for him and his truth. God is honoured when hearts are changed by the Holy Spirit through the word. God is magnified by lives that demonstrate that they delight in all that he is and all that he has done. This is how God is glorified in sermons, talks and Bible studies.

How to get it wrong

It follows that God is not glorified in talks that don't have these sorts of priorities as their chief goal. He's not honoured in the Bible study which is just the sharing of ignorance rather than really getting at what God is saying said. He's not glorified in the sermon that simply ignores the difficult or controversial bits. And neither is he glorified in the talk that is accurate but merely educational. It is love that builds up. Mere knowledge only puffs up. The endpoint we're aiming at is *not* education. It's transformation and worship.

There's a feeling in some places today that Bible teaching should not be the core component of corporate Christian life. People think that somehow it doesn't connect. It doesn't feel as if it meets people's felt needs. When we hear this we wonder if people have really grasped what the Bible actually is—God's very word written. But we also wonder if they've been done a disservice by having to sit through Bible studies that were an irrelevance or worse.

The aim of all exegesis (working out what the Bible text is saying) is to introduce people to God so that he is glorified. So talks that just stop at exegesis and never go any further not only fail to be good talks, they also fail to be good exegesis because they don't urge people to the end point that exegesis requires. Some people say that if you just understand the passage, it will somehow lead to obedience automatically. *We disagree.* It's possible to understand a passage by logic alone and for there to be no adoration in it at all.

So don't prepare talks quickly or shabbily. God wants worship. The Bible is calling people from all nations to turn from their idolatry, and worship the true and living God. Our desire is for preaching saturated with the presence of God. Martyn Lloyd-Jones says the chief end of preaching is "to give men and women a sense of God and his presence." [1] He goes on: "I can forgive the preacher almost anything if he gives me a sense of God, if he gives me something for my soul, if he gives me the sense that, though he is inadequate in himself, he is handling something which is very great and very glorious, if he gives me some dim glimpse of the majesty and the glory of God, the love of Christ my Saviour, and the magnificence of the Gospel. If he does that I am his debtor, and I am profoundly grateful to him." [2]

Our task is to light fires of worship in people's hearts. We are Spirit-filled Bible arsonists! Psalm 119 v 129-136 says:

> Your statutes are wonderful;
>   therefore I obey them.

1 D. Martyn Lloyd-Jones, *Preaching and Preachers*, Zondervan, 2011, p110.

2 D. Martyn Lloyd Jones, *Preachers and Preaching*, p110-111.

The unfolding of your words gives light;
it gives understanding to the simple.
I open my mouth and pant,
longing for your commands.
Turn to me and have mercy on me,
as you always do to those who love your name.
Direct my footsteps according to your word;
let no sin rule over me.
Redeem me from human oppression,
that I may obey your precepts.
Make your face shine on your servant
and teach me your decrees.
Streams of tears flow from my eyes,
for your law is not obeyed.

Our job is to take the desires of verses like these and enact them publicly before people. We want people who obey because they're seized with the wonder of God's word. We want people who are wise because they recognise their limitations and his wisdom. We want people who experience God's mercy because his word has convinced them of his character. We want people who follow God's ways and know power over sin because they've tasted that the Lord is good.

Our job is to **preach the glory of God for the glory of God**. The glory of God is both the content and goal of our preaching. Life is not about me. And preaching is not all about addressing my needs. Creation and redemption are all about God and his glory. We're to lift people's sight above the horizons of their small me-centred world to see the majesty of God. But here's the thing: the glory of God is the water that truly satisfies and the rock upon which we can build our lives.

So planning a good sermon or Bible study means working first on exposing people to God in his word (exposition) and then, secondly, on inviting them to worship the God who there reveals himself. The first step of understanding the text is vital. But the danger is that we put all our time into doing this first task and never get round to planning how to turn from text to application and adoration.

Preaching is among the most glorious tasks that a person can do in this world. As you're sitting at your desk with your Bible open, jotting down ideas, you're preparing for God to burst open hearts with his word and bring gospel transformation. It's not a small task!

Our first three principles are in a sense all variations on one theme. Our goal is not simply education. Our goal is to present Christ as we discover him in the Scriptures so that affections are won for him so that lives are changed and God is glorified. At the end of our sermons we want hearers whose hearts are filled with adoration for God, so much so that they offer their lives in worship to him as a living sacrifice.

Questions for reflection

Ask an experienced preacher to reflect with you on a recent sermon which they have preached. It might be a sermon you've heard in your church or you might listen to a recording. If you're meeting as a group, they could preach it to you. Discuss with them:

- The original context in which it was delivered.
- How they arrived at this understanding of the passage.
- How they arrived at the main application.
- How they arrived at this sermon structure.
- The process of preparation.
- Their normal preaching practices.
- How they evaluate whether or not it was a good sermon.

Ideas for action

Worship over the text

We have seen that our job is preach the glory of God for the glory of God. It follows, then, that the number one principle for preparing to preach is this: *worship over the text*. It's infinitely more important than sermon structures or good Bible study questions or rhetorical devices.

Bow the knees of your heart before the throne of heaven and say:

> "Father, you have given me a mighty task and I'm not the equal of it. Give me such a willing heart to learn what is written here and to worship and obey you in it, that what spills over into my preaching is not my knowledge so much as my delight in the Lord."

God is honoured by prayer like that. And people will spot the difference between preaching you deliver because you have to and preaching you deliver because your heart is full of the splendour of God.

Pray through the text.

Take a verse or two at a time (or an episode at a time if you're working on a story) and the turn this into prayer.

Rejoice. Repent. Request.

The living God speaks to us through his word. Turn that speech into a two-way conversation.

PART TWO

THE MEANS OF PREACHING

4 THE WORD OF GOD

Principle

Effective preachers trust in the authority of the Bible.

Consider this

Pete and Heather had just come back from a big Christian conference. "It was great", they gushed. "The music was brilliant and the preaching was wonderful." Dwayne, their pastor, couldn't help feeling a little put out. "The main speaker was so inspiring. Everyone was really moved. I'll send you some internet links. It would be great if you could preach more like him."

A few days later Dwayne listened to a couple of the talks. He laughed. He cried. Peter and Heather were right—it was all very moving. But Dwayne felt uneasy. The speaker had looked at each verse in the passage in turn. But he'd mostly then pointed to cross-references or told stories. Somehow something was missing.

"Did you listen to those links I sent you?" Pete asked the following Sunday.

"Yes," said Dwayne. "And he was very inspiring. But…"

Bible background
Read 2 Timothy 3 v 14 – 4 v 5

- Look at 3 v 15-16. What is the Bible?
- Look at 3 v 16-17. What does the Bible do? Can you give examples from your life of the Bible working in the ways described in these verses?
- Look at 4 v 2. We're to "correct, rebuke and encourage". Which of these is strong in your public preaching and personal exhortation? Which is weak?
- Look at 4 v 2. What might it mean for you to preach "with great patience and careful instruction"?
- Look at 4 v 3-5. What are the threats to the preaching of the word in your situation?

Read all about it

If we don't share the convictions the Bible has about itself, then we'll read the bits we want to read and ignore the bits we don't like. We'll place other religious activity on the same level as the Bible. We'll see the Bible as a book about me rather than about God. This leads to a therapeutic picking of favourite passages because they speak subjectively to our experience. We'll think working hard to understand the Bible is boring. We'll assume references to "you" are written directly to "me" personally, without thinking about the original readers.

These attitudes lead us away from approaching God as he really is. Where that slippage happens, there is impoverished discipleship and mission that offers nothing concrete because the authority of God over our lives has been side-lined. Saying that you are simply sharing your thoughts rather than presuming to speak on behalf of God might appear a humble attitude. But in fact your implicit claim is that your own ideas are worth people's attention. "If anyone speaks, they should do so as one who speaks the very words of God" (1 Peter 4 v 11).

So what convictions should we bring to teaching Scripture?

God speaks in the Bible about himself

What do we mean by "God's word"?

- God's Word is God's Son (John 1 v 1-3).
- God's word is God's book, the Bible (Hebrews 4 v 12).
- God's word is God's gospel (Philippians 2 v 16).

All these three senses belong together. God has revealed himself in himself. The Son of God is God. "The Word was God." So what we see is what we get. There's no secret God hidden by his revelation. The Bible is the record and explanation of God's revelation in his Son. And again the Bible is a divine act. It is the Spirit-breathed word. This means that to the extent that what we say is faithful to the Bible, we speak "the very words of God" (1 Peter 4 v 11). The Bible is much more a book about God than a book about us. First and foremost it is God telling us about God. But it is also God telling us how we can know him, relate to him and live as his people in the world.

God speaks in the Bible without error

Because it's God's word, the Bible is without error in all that it affirms. The Holy Spirit spoke through the human authors to ensure the Bible is true and reliable.

God speaks in the Bible today

The Holy Spirit not only spoke (past tense) through the writers of the Bible to ensure that what they wrote is God's word, he also speaks (present tense) to the hearers of the Bible to ensure that what we hear is God's word. And the Holy Spirit speaks now in the present when the Bible is read and taught. The word of God comes on the breath of God. The Spirit opens our hearts so the words are a living message from God.

To give an example, in Romans 9 v 17 Paul quotes what God said (in the past), but introduces it as what Scripture says (in the present). Again, in Romans 9 v 25-26 he quotes what Hosea wrote (in the past), but introduces it as what God says (in the present). If people assume that Scripture was God's word only in the past, they need to look elsewhere to find God's word for today.

God speaks in the Bible to change the world

I can do things with my words. When I book a ticket over the phone there's no difference between my words acting and me acting. This is even more true of God's words. God acts through his words. His words make things happen. This means we should expect the word to have a transforming effect in our lives. It should be changing us by the Holy Spirit's power into the likeness of Jesus.

Consider as an example John 15 v 3:

> You are already clean because of the word I have spoken to you.

We can be clean through the word Jesus spoke to his disciples. He is still speaking that word in and through the Bible. We're not sanctified (made pure like Christ) through some new word or new act. We're sanctified as God acts through his eternal word. Jesus, presented to us in the Bible, is the means by which we know God and receive eternal life.

So we should never divide God from the Bible. It's hard enough to separate my words from me, because they convey who I am and what

I think. This is even more true of God. I can lie so my words misrepresent me. But God reveals himself in his Son, the Word of God, and the Spirit has ensured that the Bible is the accurate and authoritative record of this revelation. So when the Bible is read and taught, what is happening is nothing less than God's voice being heard. Without it there is no revelation from God, no authentic spirituality and no relationship with God.

How does this relate practically to you and your church? In 2 Timothy 3 v 15-17 Paul says it is the Scriptures which make people "wise for salvation through faith in Christ Jesus" and it is through the Scriptures "that the servant of God may be thoroughly equipped for every good work". In the light of these convictions, Paul goes on to give Timothy a solemn exhortation:

> In the presence of God and of Christ Jesus, who will judge the living and the dead, and in view of his appearing and his kingdom, I give you this charge: Preach the word; be prepared in season and out of season; correct, rebuke and encourage—with great patience and careful instruction. **2 Timothy 4 v 1-2**

In the light of eternity and in the light of the coming judgment, we're to preach the word patiently and carefully to believers and unbelievers. We're to correct, rebuke and encourage. We're to keep our heads even when people don't want to hear God's word (4 v 3-5).

So what you say must be seen to come from the text. Your application, too, must come from the text rather than being added on by you. John Stott says:

> To expound Scripture is to bring out of the text what is there and expose it to view. The expositor prises open what appears to be closed, makes plain what is obscure, unravels what is knotted and unfolds what is tightly packed. The opposite of exposition is "imposition", which is to impose on the text what is not there ...

> In expository preaching the biblical text is neither a conventional introduction to a sermon on a largely different theme, nor a convenient peg on which to hang a ragbag of miscellaneous thoughts, but a master which dictates and controls what is said.[1]

> We must do our utmost to ensure that it speaks to our time, but not bowdlerise it in order to secure a fake relevance. Our calling is to be faithful and relevant, not merely trendy.[2]

Avoid displays of scholarship. A key question to ask is: *will people have more confidence that they can read the Bible for themselves after your sermon or less?* If you build your interpretation on extra-biblical information, then the answer will be less. If you refer to lots of scholars (however orthodox), then the answer will be less. If you frequently refer to what the Hebrew or Greek "actually" says, then the answer will be less.

If your sermons are full of your experience, your wisdom, your scholarship, your advice and your stories, then they will carry the authority of you. If you're a wise and godly person, then that authority may be significant. People may listen to you with respect. But your authority is nothing compared to God's authority! And if your sermons are full of God's word, then you will speak with the authority of God.

The apostle Paul says:

> Do your best to present yourself to God as one approved, a worker who does not need to be ashamed and who correctly handles the word of truth. **2 Timothy 2 v 15**

1 John Stott, *Between Two Worlds*, Eerdmans, 1982, p125-126.
2 John Stott, *The Contemporary Christian* in *The Essential John Stott*, IVP, 1992, p361.

Questions for reflection

Speaking beyond your experience

How can a man without children speak on parenting? How can a man with children speak on childlessness?

Topical preaching

Topical preaching starts with the questions of the culture and shows how the Bible speaks to those issues. Expository preaching (preaching that carefully explains a particular passage of Scripture) and preaching through books of the Bible starts with the agenda of God's word and shows how it speaks to us today. You can, of course, preach topical sermons by expounding Bible passages. But if you don't preach through Bible books from different genres, then you're never letting the Bible set the agenda.

What do you think is an appropriate balance between topical preaching and preaching through books of the Bible?

Imagine a diet of cake. You might think it sounds like fun, but we all know it's not going to make you healthy. In the same way congregations need a balanced diet. We need to preach the whole counsel of God. That means we need a good mix of:

- sermons on Old Testament and New Testament
- sermons on different biblical genres
- sermons covering large sections and sermons interacting with a few verses

Ideas for action

The authority of the Bible needs not only to be a foundational conviction. It should be reflected in what you say and how you say it.

1. Preach the message of the passage not other similar passages

Preach the passage in front of you. Don't preach, for example, what's not in your passage, but in parallel passages—unless you're drawing attention to those differences to highlight the distinctive message of your passage. Use cross-references to explain your passage, not to supplement it. Why? Because the more you preach other passages, the more you're the one setting the agenda rather than allowing the word of God to set the agenda. What you bring in from elsewhere may be biblical, but it will be your choice and therefore your agenda.

This will also keep your preaching fresh. Different passages and books present the truth in different ways. If you flatten this out by always cross-referencing then you're preaching will be repetitive and bland. It's lazy to preach the truth from one passage in the same way you would preach it (or have preached it) from another passage. Let the colour and texture of Scripture gives your sermons colour and texture. The great nineteenth century preacher Charles Spurgeon says:

> *The surest way to maintain variety is to keep to the mind of the Holy Spirit in the particular passage under consideration. No two texts are exactly similar; something in the connection or drift of the passage gives to each apparently identical text a shade of difference. Keep to the Spirit's track and you will never repeat yourself or be short of matter.*[1]

1 Charles H. Spurgeon, *Lectures to My Students*, Zondervan, 1954, p73.

2. *Preach the message of the passage not just the words of the passage*

People often think they're doing exposition because they go through a passage verse by verse. But in fact they're merely doing a kind of word-association exercise in which words or phrases in the passage prompt thoughts or stories or applications. Instead we need to be grappling with the message the author intended to convey to his readers. Here are some dangers:

- *The passage shapes the theme, but not the content.* The preacher notes what the passage is about and then preaches some thoughts on that topic, without really showing what the passage itself says on the topic.
- *The passage shapes the content, but not the structure.* The preacher explains what the passage is saying, but doesn't engage with how the passage says it.
- *The passage shapes the structure, but not the theme.* The preacher gives some thoughts on each verse in turn, but without wrestling with the overall argument of the passage.

Can you think of examples of these approaches that you have heard—or given yourself?

5 THE SPIRIT OF GOD

Principle

Effective preachers trust in the power of the Spirit.

Consider this

Bob looked at the passage. He was fairly confident he understood its main message. But how did it speak to his congregation? After all, no-one in his congregation was claiming Christians should be circumcised!

He didn't want to give a lecture on first-century Christianity. He wanted his congregation to really engage with God's word. He knew something of the struggles some were facing. He felt the complacency of others. He wanted to encourage his people, lift them, challenge them, excite them. But how? What should he do? He reached for his commentaries.

As usual, Bob had done the bulk of work on his sermon on Monday. On Friday he'd had another look at it and made a few changes. Now it was 8.00 am on Sunday morning. He had just over an hour before he needed to leave the house. One last chance to prepare to preach. What should he do? He turned on his computer to give his sermon one final edit before he printed it off.

Bible background
Read 1 Corinthians 2 v 1-16

- **Look at 2 v 4-5.** Persuasive words persuade so what's the problem with relying on eloquence in our preaching?

- **Look at 2 v 4-5, 10, 13-16.** How are people persuaded by the message of the cross?

Read all about it

Many preachers don't expect supernatural activity to accompany their preaching. Or, if we do, we expect it to involve changing people's minds in an unseen way. We're content when people have understood facts from the text. We don't expect our preaching to lead to joyful adoration, heart-felt thanksgiving or lives that are changed because people have been assaulted by God's glory. We don't expect miracles to accompany our preaching (except perhaps unseen changes of conviction).

Jonathan Edwards commented on how easy it is to default to low expectations of God working:

> How greatly has the doctrine of the inward experience or sensible perceiving of the immediate power and operation of the Spirit of God, been reproached and ridiculed by many of late! They say, the manner of the Spirit of God, is to co-operate in a silent, secret, and undiscernible way with the use of means, and our own endeavours; so that there is no distinguishing by sense, between the influences of the Spirit of God, and the natural operations of the faculties of our own minds.[1]

1 Jonathan Edwards, *The Religious Affections*, Banner of Truth, 1961, Pt. 2, Section IV, p65.

Paul's expectations were very different. According to Romans 15, when he preached he expected:

- people to be sanctified by the Holy Spirit (v 16).
- Christ to accomplish the task of leading people to obey God (v 18).
- evident manifestations of the power of the Spirit (v 19).

All of this he describes as having "fulfilled the ministry of the gospel of Christ" (v 19, ESV).

Let's not fall into the trap of thinking that because our preaching is not accompanied by a great deal of evident supernatural activity, we shouldn't expect it today. Let's not justify our lack of power by doubting God's power. Instead, let's fall on our knees and beseech him; so that, like Paul, our preaching might come "not simply with words, but also with power, with the Holy Spirit and deep conviction" (1 Thessalonians 1 v 5).

1 Peter 1 v 12 talks about "the things that have now been told you by those who have preached the gospel to you by the Holy Spirit sent from heaven". There are two people speaking when biblical preaching is going on: the human speaker ("those who have preached the gospel to you") and the Holy Spirit. Preaching is done by people, by the Holy Spirit. The result is that people are "born again ... through the living and enduring word of God" and people have "tasted that the Lord is good" (1 Peter 1 v 23 – 2 v 3).

So here are a couple of preaching tips from the Apostle Paul.

1. Trust the message of the cross

First, Paul says *we must trust a message that people think is foolish*. "The message of the cross is foolishness to those who are perishing, but to us who are being saved it is the power of God" (1 Corinthians 1 v 18).

> For I resolved to know nothing while I was with you except Jesus Christ and him crucified. **1 Corinthians 2 v 2**

To the natural mind the message of the cross is foolish (1 Corinthians 1 v 18; 2 v 14). In no age has it been considered wise by worldly standards. Today people claim it's outdated, irrelevant, morally repellent or even barbaric. Don't preach the cross if you want to be popular! Preach instead a universalism that removes the judgment revealed at the cross. Or preach sermons full of jokes and anecdotes that entertain your hearers, or make your focus all on self-improvement, or promise prosperity in this life. These will make your preaching popular. But they all lack the power of God (1 v 17-18). Through the cross, God refutes all human pride and all human attempts at self-salvation. So trust the message of the cross. You might not enjoy it. It will open you up to ridicule and scorn. *Get used to it.* God is using the foolish things to shame the wise.

2. *Trust the power of the Spirit*

> My message and my preaching were not with wise and persuasive words, but with a demonstration of the Spirit's power, so that your faith might not rest on human wisdom, but on God's power.
>
> **1 Corinthians 2 v 4-5**

What made Paul's preaching effective was not his eloquence or persuasion, *but the Spirit's power.* Preach the cross without using eloquent words. That doesn't mean we shouldn't prepare—we want to portray the glory of God in Christ as best we can.

What it means is this. If you use eloquent words because you want your presentation to look good, then *you'll point to yourself but not to the cross.* If you enjoy public exposure or the sound of your own voice then beware: you may be emptying the cross of its power. If people are persuaded by your eloquence, then they may also be persuaded to abandon Christianity by someone who's more eloquent. But if they experience the power of the Holy Spirit, they're a new person.

So don't rely on yourself, but on the Holy Spirit. If you want to see the Spirit using you in power, then humble yourself and pray. Charles Spurgeon used to pray on every step up to his pulpit: "I believe in the Holy Spirit". And it was a very high pulpit with a lot of steps! John Stott says:

> "I have always found it helpful to do as much of my sermon preparation as possible on my knees, with the Bible open before me, in prayerful study."[1] He says you should pray that you will "so possess the message that the message possesses you ... We need to pray until our text comes freshly alive to us, the glory shines forth from it, the fire burns in our heart, and we begin to experience the explosive power of God's Word within us." [2]

Likewise St Augustine said:

> [A preacher] should be in no doubt that any ability he has and however much he has derives more from his devotion to prayer than his dedication to oratory; and so, by praying for himself and for those he is about to address, he must become a man of prayer before becoming a man of words.[3]

And don't worry if you feel weak or you're terrified every time you have to preach. That's ok. It's ok because God uses weak people rather than strong people.

If it was ok for Paul to come with fear and trembling, then it's ok for you to come with fear and trembling too (1 Corinthians 2 v 3-5). Self-confident people attract glory to themselves. Weak people demonstrate that the power lies with God. "Let the one who boasts boast in the Lord" (1 Corinthians 1 v 31).

When you preach, do you want people to say: "He's a great preacher" or "He's a great Saviour"?

---

1 Condensed from John R. W. Stott, *Between Two Worlds*, 211-216.
2 Condensed from John R. W. Stott, *Between Two Worlds*, 211-216.
3 St Augustine, *On Christian Teaching*, OUP, 1997, 121.

Ideas for Action

Depend on the Spirit in your preparation

- *How long do you spend in preparation before you preach?*
- *How long do you spend in prayer before you preach?*

Of course, we can't measure our self-reliance simply by comparing the time we spend in preparation with the time in prayer. God doesn't need persuading by lengthy prayers. But our commitment to prayer is a recognition and sign of our dependence on God. Do you pray for your preaching in a way that shows you're relying on the God's power?

A famous preacher was asked about a sermon illustration that had really driven home his message to the congregation. "How did he find it?" he was asked. "It came to me in prayer," he replied. "My preparation was stuck so I prayed." "For how long?" "About two hours." *Do you pray as your prepare?*

Depend on the Spirit in your preaching

This how John Piper describes how he practices a dependence on the Holy Spirit in preaching.[1]

> There are five steps that I follow in seeking to preach not in my own strength but in the strength that God supplies. I sum them up with an acronym so that I can remember them when my mind is befogged by fear or distraction. The acronym is *APTAT*.
>
> Picture me in the front pew at Bethlehem Baptist Church. Two minutes remain before I stand to preach. One of the elders or an apprentice steps to the pulpit to read the text for the morning message before I come. As he begins to read, I bow my head before the Lord for one last transaction

1 John Piper, *The Supremacy of God in Preaching*, Baker, 2004, p47-49.

before the sacred moment of preaching. I almost always put my heart through *APTAT* before the Lord.

1. **I ADMIT** to the Lord that without him I can do nothing. I affirm that John 15 v 5 is absolutely true of me at this moment: "Apart from me you can do nothing." I admit to God: My heart would not beat without you. My eyes could not see without you. My memory would fail without you. Without you I will be plagued with distraction and self-consciousness. Without you I will doubt your reality. Without you I will not love the people. Without you I will feel no awe at the truth I am about to speak. Without you the Word will fall on deaf ears. Who but you can raise the dead? Without you, O God, I can do nothing.

2. Therefore, Father, **I PRAY** for help. I beg for the insight and the power and the humility and the love and the memory and the freedom that I need to preach this message for the glory of your name and the gladness of your people and the ingathering of your elect. I accept your invitation, "Call upon me in the day of trouble; I will deliver you and you shall glorify me." (Psalm 50 v 15).
   And I should perhaps mention that this is not the beginning of my prayer for this sermon. Its preparation was done in almost constant prayer for help, and I get up three and a half hours before the first service to spend two hours getting my heart as ready as I can before I come to the church. And during that time I search for a promise in the Word that will be the basis of the next step in *APTAT* in those last minutes.

3. The next step is **TRUST**—not merely in a general way in God's goodness, but in a specific promise where I can bank

my hope for that hour. I find this kind of specific trust in a particular Word of God utterly essential to fight off the assault of Satan in those moments. Recently I strengthened myself with Psalm 40 v 17: "As for me I am poor and needy, but the Lord takes thought for me. You are my help and my deliverer; do not delay, O my God!" I memorize the verse early in the morning, recite it to myself in that moment, believe it, resist the devil with it, and...

4. **I ACT** in the confidence that God will fulfil his Word. And I can testify that, though the fulness of blessing that I long to see has been delayed, God has met me and my people again and again in the display of his glory and the glad submission of his people. This leads to the final step.

5. **I THANK** God at the end of the message that I was sustained and that the truth of his Word and the purchase of his cross have been preached in some measure in the power of his Spirit to the glory of his name.

And I dream that in twenty years some forty-two-year-old preacher will stand in his pulpit with a ministry a hundred times as fruitful as mine and say, "John Piper never knew it, but when I sat under his preaching, the glory of God and the cross of Christ and the power of the Spirit were irresistible, and God called me to the ministry of the Word."

6 THE PREACHER

Principle

Effective preachers trust in the character of God.

Consider this

It was Sunday evening and Ryan felt terrible. Three people had come up to him after his sermon to complain.

One of them had said they thought his sermon had been a bit harsh. "I know that's what the Bible teaches," they'd said, "but there's no need to be so insistent about it." "Perhaps I should tone it down," he thought. "After all, I need to start were people are."

But what really rankled with him were the other two comments. They'd both complained that he'd gone on too long. He'd worked so hard on his preparation. All his preaching heroes spoke for around an hour, but he couldn't keep people's attention for 20 minutes. He just wanted to give up.

The phone rang. "How did it go today?" He recognised the voice. It was Carlos, his mentor. "It was a disaster," Ryan said and for ten minutes all his frustrations came out. Finally there was a pause. Then Carlos said…

Bible background
Read 1 Thessalonians 2 v 1-16

- Where does Paul look for his approval?
- What's Paul's attitude to his hearers?
- What will preaching be like if the preacher is "trying to please people" (v 2-7)?
- What will preaching be like if the preacher doesn't care about his hearers (v 8-9)?
- What does it mean for a preacher to be like a mother to his hearers (v 7)?
- What does it mean to be like a father (v 11-12)?
- Paul shared his life with people as well as the gospel (v 8). What might this mean in your context?

Read all about it
God's chosen method for communicating his life-giving word is people like you and me. His infallible word is entrusted to fallible people. The means by which God changes lives is the word of God proclaimed by the people of God through the Spirit of God.

Personality
Preaching is, as the nineteenth-century American preacher, Phillips Brooks famously said: "truth through personality". It's an amazing thought. Preaching is not just truth. It's also personality. Of course there's a danger that personality obscures the truth and preaching becomes all about the preacher. But your distinctive style, experi-

ence and character are used by God to give colour and texture to the message.

When you start out as a preacher, it's a good idea to model yourself on preachers you admire. But over time you should let your own personality come through and develop your own style. God didn't make you to be just a clone of your heroes; and if you only try to preach like them, you'll fail to preach well. God made you with a distinctive personality, and you should preach in a way that reflects that personality.

Gifting

Preaching is a spiritual gift. We don't need the mediation of a priest as people did in the Old Testament for together we are a royal priesthood. Jeremiah promises: "'No longer will a man teach his neighbour, or a man his brother, saying, "Know the LORD," because they will all know me, from the least of them to the greatest,"'declares the LORD." (Jeremiah 31 v 34) But God has given teachers and preachers to the church to help us understand his word better and to encourage us to love him more.

This doesn't mean other Christians can't encourage other one another with the word or proclaim the gospel to their friends. Every Christian is called to "speak the truth in love" to one another. But God also especially equips some to be pastor-teachers (Ephesians 4 v 11-16)—just as we are all called to serve others, but the New Testament also talks about a special gift of service.

"Do you understand what you are reading?" Philip asks the Ethiopian eunuch in Acts 8 v 30-31. "'How can I,' he said, 'unless someone explains it to me?'" God has given teachers and preachers to his church. You're probably reading this book because you're one of those people and you want to think about how you can exercise your gift better.

Character

Your personality and gifting are important. But more important than both is the *character* of the preacher. God's word has power because it's God's word breathed by God's Spirit. But you're preaching will have a bigger impact on your hearers if your word and your life match up.

This doesn't mean you need to be faultless before you can preach effectively. Then there would be no preachers! Praise God, our message is not salvation by good works, but by Christ's good work and God's grace. People need to see that when preachers are tempted and when we sin, we turn to Christ in faith and repentance. People need to see God's grace having an impact in our lives. Paul tells Timothy to model not perfection, but "progress" (1 Timothy 4 v 15).

Justification by preaching

The greatest threat to your preaching is not a lack of skill, but a lack of repentance and faith. Consider what happens if you're not embracing the truth about God.

God is great

If you don't believe that God is in control, then you'll want to feel as if you're in control when you preach. You'll rely on your own study or insight or eloquence instead of relying on the Holy Spirit. Or you may well have too much material (just in case). Or you'll feel the need to be in control of the outcomes, pressuring people into a response. Remember, too, that the new understanding you've gained has come after hours of preparation and perhaps months of consideration. So don't be too frustrated if the congregation don't get it after 30 minutes! Faith in the sovereignty of God enables you to be patient with people and give them time to change.

God is glorious

If you worry about what people think of you, then you may refrain from challenging them to repent. You'll give them what "their itching ears want to hear" (2 Timothy 4 v 3-5). Or, in another context, you may want to impress people with your orthodoxy and so present the truth without any pastoral sensitivity. It depends on who it is you want to impress. You may over-prepare, spending hours creating a perfect sermon so people think of you as a great preacher. As a result you may waste time you could spend serving God in other (perhaps unseen) ways. The answer to this fear of man is the fear of God, to recognise that God is the glorious One and it's his opinion that matters.

God is good

If you're not finding joy in God, then you won't want to do the hard work of preparation and prayer. You'll under-prepare because you're looking for joy elsewhere. As you sit down to work on your sermon, you'll easily be distracted by the latest news or blog posts or Twitter or Facebook—anything but the hard work of preparation. You may offer a dry explanation of the passage on the one hand or fill your sermons with entertaining stories on the other hand, because in both cases the truth didn't excite you in preparation so you have nothing to offer.

God is gracious

Preachers can easily try to find their identity in preaching rather than in Christ. If this is what you do, then how you feel on Monday morning will depend on how it went on Sunday morning: a good response and you'll be full of pride; a poor response and you'll be despondent. You may exalt the status of the public sermon, making your role the centre of church life, because your identity is invested in this position. Again, because your identity is invested in the fruit of your preaching, you may pressure people into a response. It's all too easy for preachers to preach justification by grace even as they themselves are practising justification by preaching!

Questions for reflection

Consider what might happen if a preacher did not embrace each of these truths. How would it affect their preaching?

- **God is great**—*so we do not have to be in control*

- **God is glorious**—*so we do not have to fear others*

- **God is good**—*so we do not have to look elsewhere*

- **God is gracious**—*so we do not have to prove ourselves*

- *Which of these is a danger to you?*

PART THREE

THE CONTENT OF PREACHING

7 PREACHING GOOD NEWS

Principle

Because the gospel is good news, your sermon should be good news.

Consider this

I (Tim) grew up in a church tradition in which many churches had a "gospel sermon" on Sunday evenings. This "gospel sermon" usually involved preaching about God's grace and Christ's work on the cross.

The *hope* was that unbelievers would put their faith in Christ and be saved (though as it happens there were rarely any unbelievers at this meeting).

The *implication* was that the sermon in the morning was not a gospel sermon. This sermon was for believers and in it they were told how they should live.

The *gospel* was preached to unbelievers in the hope they might be saved. God's *law* was preached to believers so they knew how to live in obedience to God.

What's wrong with this picture?

Bible background

Read Colossians 1 v 15-23

- How does Paul define the gospel that he serves (1 v 15-23)?

- How do we continue in our faith (1 v 23)?

Read Colossians 2 v 6-7

- How do we start the Christian life and how do we continue (2 v 6-7)?

Read Colossians 2 v 20 – 3 v 10

- What does a set of rules appear to produce in someone's life?

- What does a set of rules actually produce in someone's life?

- How do we get rid of wrong behaviour?

Read all about it

Writing to the Corinthians Paul says:

> Now, brothers and sisters, I want to remind you of the gospel I preached to you, which you received and on which you have taken your stand. By this gospel you are saved, if you hold firmly to the word I preached to you. Otherwise, you have believed in vain.
>
> **1 Corinthians 15 v 1-2**

What do we preach? We preach the gospel. The gospel is not just for unbelievers. It's not just what initially saves us. Paul urges the

Corinthians to "hold firmly to the word I preached to you". It is the gospel of Christ Jesus as Lord that sustains Christians and grows Christians and equips Christians.

> So then, just as you received Christ Jesus as Lord, continue to live your lives in him, rooted and built up in him, strengthened in the faith as you were taught, and overflowing with thankfulness.
>
> **Colossians 2 v 6-7**

The message that saved us is the message that we continue to live. We never graduate from the gospel to some higher teacher.

Nothing controversial in this. Yet it's all too easy to preach something other than the gospel.

We might preach **ourselves** (2 Corinthians 4 v 5). We might fill our sermons with personal stories that serve to promote us or our "systems".

We might preach **myths that people want to hear** (2 Timothy 4 v 3-5). We might promise health and prosperity in this life instead of calling people to self-denial and self-sacrifice for Christ. There were many false prophets in the Old Testament crying "Peace, peace" when there was no peace.

We might preach **human wisdom**—perhaps a bit of pop psychology or good advice. And what you offer might genuinely be good advice. But it will only have the authority of your wisdom. It won't have the authority of God. And it won't have the power of God. It might improve someone's life (and it might not), but it won't change their heart or save their soul.

But perhaps the main alternative which we might be tempted to adopt, or to which we might default, is **preaching law**. After all, there's a lot of it in the Bible!

You would think good evangelical, justification-by-faith people would not do this. But we do! Law says: *"You should... You should not sleep with your boyfriend. You should read your Bible every day. You should not get drunk. You should witness to your friends. You should not lose your temper."* That's not good news. Not to someone struggling with those issues. It is condemnation.

What the gospel says is this: Jesus is better and therefore: *"You need not... You need not get drunk because Jesus offers a better refuge. You need not lose your temper because God is in control of the situation.* That's good news! Sin makes promises. The gospel exposes those promises as false promises and points to a God who is bigger and better than anything sin offers. That is good news.

- Don't say *"You should not..."*. Instead say: *"You need not... because..."*
- Don't say *"You should..."*. Instead say *"You can... because..."*

But what about all that law in the Bible? All those commands? All those warnings of judgment?

The law was an expression of God's liberating rule

The law of Moses described how God's old-covenant people were to live under the liberating rule of God. God is not a tyrant and his will is not a burden.

Imagine being one of the freed slaves gathered at Mount Sinai. All your life you've been a slave under Pharaoh's rule, with continual work and no rights over your life or property. And then you hear the command to keep the Sabbath and the command not to murder or steal. You're going to say: "That's a great idea. I love the sound of that." The law of Moses was designed to create a beautiful community that showed to the nations the goodness of God. The law of Moses became a burden when people thought of it as the way to earn God's approval.

The law pointed God's people to the Saviour

The Israelites couldn't keep the law of Moses because they (like us) were sinners. But that was no cause for despair because the law included the sacrificial system that offered provision for sin (at least in a prophetic sense).

So the law led them to the gospel by removing false self-confidence, and driving them to God's mercy and the need for God to provide a

Saviour. "But now," says Paul in Romans 3 v 21, "apart from law the righteousness of God has been made known, to which the Law and the Prophets testify."

So when we preach Old Testament law passages from the Bible, we can and should point to the Saviour who frees us from the curse of the law. Indeed, that was the law's basic purpose according to Romans 3, Galatians 3 and Hebrews 7 – 8.

Here's the test of whether your sermon is a gospel sermon. **Is it good news?**

After all, the word "gospel" means "good news". Our sermons must all sound like good news to people. They should leave genuinely glad people thinking: "What I've just heard is such good news".

That doesn't mean we go soft on the challenge of the gospel. The gospel produces a response of faith and repentance, so every sermon is a call to faith and repentance. We call on people to turn away from their selfishness and idolatry, and to turn towards faith in God.

But we're also realistic. Sometimes people will feel the challenge of the sermon and miss the note of gospel. Of course it should have been there, loud and clear. When we call people away from the temptations of sin, we're always calling *to* something better. We're calling them to a life lived with God and for God. We're calling them to his liberating rule. We're calling them to the glory of God in the face of Jesus. We're calling them to the love of God revealed on the cross. We're calling them to a better option.

Our sermons should never leave people who are hungering for God feeling condemned. Why not? Because "there is now no condemnation for those who are in Christ Jesus" (Romans 8 v 1). Half way through the sermon they may feel condemned. But *never* by the end. Whenever we show people their sin, we must always also show them their Saviour.

Questions for reflection

- What's the difference between a sermon that challenges people and a sermon that condemns people?

- **Look at Exodus 19 – 20.** How would you preach the gospel from the story of the giving of the ten commandments?

- Imagine you're preaching a sermon on abortion. How might you ensure this sermon was heard as good news?

- Review a recent sermon. How did it offer people good news? What was the call to repentance? What was the call to faith?

8 PREACHING CHRIST

Principle

Because the whole Bible points to Christ, your sermon should point to Christ.

Consider this

I (Tim) was preparing to preach on the life of David so I listened to a number of online sermons, and was surprised by the variety of approaches I found. Here's a selection:

- One sermon described how David had to make some **hard decisions.** Sometimes he made principled choices and sometimes he had to make pragmatic choices. We, too, often have to make hard decisions so let's pray for the Spirit to give us wisdom.
- Another described how David faced **perplexing times of adversity.** The preacher then invited us to turn elsewhere in Scripture to see how we can cope in such situations.
- Yet another sermon on David's defeat of Goliath **warned against using David as an example for us**. David represents Jesus, who has defeated our enemies for us.
- One sermon series retold each story in the life of David with helpful explanatory comments.

What are the strengths and weaknesses of these approaches?

How would you preach the life of David?

Bible background
Read Luke 24 v 13-49

- What's the content of the preaching of Jesus on the first Easter Day?
- What is his "text"?
- How do you think Jesus linked the text to his content?

Read all about it

The story of Christ[1]

The Bible is all about Jesus. In Luke 24 v 44 Jesus says: "Everything must be fulfilled that is written about me in the Law of Moses, the Prophets and the Psalms". He's talking about the Old Testament. Jesus explains how "all the Scriptures" are about him.

What is written in the Scriptures is this:

> The Messiah will suffer and rise from the dead on the third day, and repentance for the forgiveness of sins will be preached in his name to all nations, beginning at Jerusalem. **Luke 24 v 46-47**

It's not just that there are a few messianic prophecies dotted around. The *whole* Bible is about Jesus from beginning to end. In John 5 v

1 This section is adapted from Tim Chester, *From Creation to New Creation: Making sense of the whole Bible Story*, The Good Book Company, 2nd Ed., 2010, p 5-15.

39-40 Jesus says: "You study the Scriptures diligently because you think that in them you have eternal life. These are the very Scriptures that testify about me, yet you refuse to come to me to have life."

Most people read detective novels from beginning to end, pitting their wits against the author, trying to pick up the clues to work out "whodunnit". But some people like to read the last chapter first. They want to know from the beginning how it will end. Then, as they read the rest of the book, it makes sense straight away. As Christians we should read the Bible—and especially the Old Testament—in that second way. We read it all the time through Jesus Christ so we can make sense of it as we go along. He is the primary context and the primary point of reference that makes sense of everything else. The first context in which to think about any Bible passage is always how God's purposes are heading towards Jesus.

There are two implications of this:

1. We need Christ to understand the Bible

Christ is the key that unlocks the meaning of the Scriptures. Thinking about how Jesus fulfils the promises and story of the Old Testament enables us to read the Old Testament as Christians.

2. We need the Old Testament to understand Christ

The New Testament writers understood Jesus in Old Testament categories. We can only fully see who Jesus is and what he's done as we see how he fulfils the Old Testament.

"Biblical theology" is the term used for this approach to the Bible. The term can be used in a wide sense to mean theology which is based on, and true to, the Bible. But it's also used in a narrower sense to mean understanding how the plotline of the Bible fits together and how it's all fulfilled in Christ. Without a sense of the whole—of the overall plan of salvation—we'll find it hard to understand the parts. And by understanding the whole, we grow in our understanding of who God is, what he's done and what he will do. And we'll also grow in our understanding of our place within those purposes. Biblical theology gives us a biblical worldview. Maybe sometimes you wish the Bible was written in the form of an encyclopaedia of theology in which you could look up God under "g" and prayer under "p". But it's not. It's a story. Understanding the big story is the only way to understand the message of the Bible. It's the way the New Testament writers used the Old Testament.

Biblical theology safeguards us from two common ways of *mis*reading the Bible, especially the Old Testament—allegorising and moralising.

Allegorising is reading a meaning into a passage from outside. Characters or events are said to represent "spiritual" truths. Allegorising by-passes the plain meaning of the words and looks instead for hidden meanings. The problem with this is the Bible can be made to mean anything at the whim of the reader. This is a very popular way of thinking today, with such interest in society in conspiracy theories, *The Da Vinci Code* and a widespread distrust of truth. God has not *hidden* truth in the Bible, but *revealed* it in a way that is open to all.

Moralising sees the stories of the Old Testament as moral tales written to instruct us. The problem with this is that they're often *immoral* tales with morally complex characters. It can be unclear whether the actions of a character are a good or bad example to us. Jephthah, for example, vows to sacrifice the first thing he sees on his return from victory, but the first thing he sees is his daughter (Judges 11). Is Jephthah a warning against rash promises or an example of devotion to God? In reality the story of the Old Testament is first and foremost God's story. Moralising by-passes Christ, reducing the message of the Bible to a message of moral rectitude rather than a message of salvation and grace.

Both allegorising and moralising involve reading into the text of Scripture something from outside. As a result we don't hear the word of God, but some other voice. Even at its best—when it's New Testament truth read into the Old Testament—it means we're not hearing the authentic voice of the Old Testament as it witnesses to

Christ. As a result our understanding and appreciation of Christ is impoverished.

This means we have to consider the continuities and discontinuities of Scripture. The Law of Moses was a two-way covenant. *If you obey I will be your God and you will be my people.* The people of Israel do disobey and so they receive the covenant curses. But in Jesus we're no longer under the Law of Moses but under grace. Jesus kept the law for us and released us from its demands. So we can't apply a passage from the Law of Moses straight to new-covenant believers without first asking: "What difference does Jesus make?" Otherwise we'll have the same applications as the synagogue next door.

So a key principle for preaching is this:

> *We need to ask how a particular text connects to Christ before we can ask how it connects to Christians in Christ.*

The following diagram might help in seeing the connections.

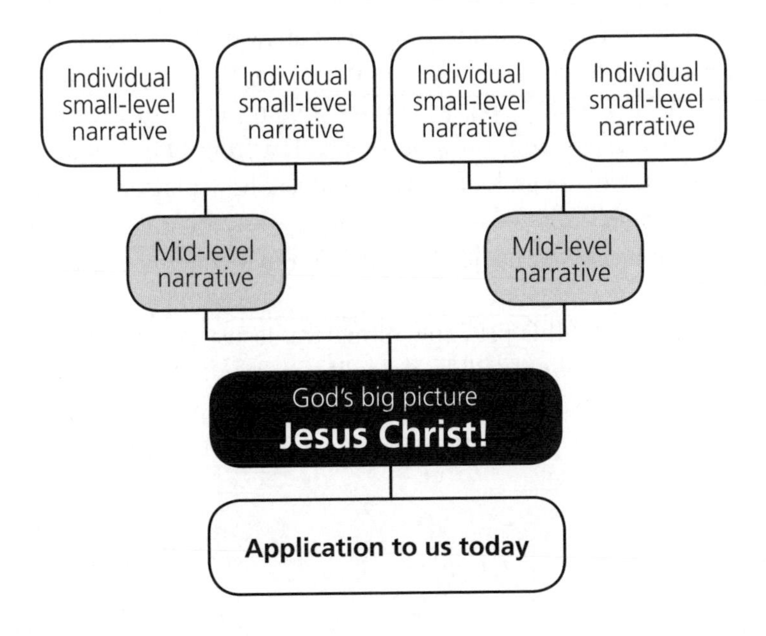

Every single episode in the Bible is there for a reason. They all contribute to a big picture of what God is doing. The question is: *how do they contribute?*

In the diagram we can see that individual narratives—the stories of individuals or particular incidents—are all included in order to contribute to some larger themes of what God is doing. These larger, mid-level narratives often circulate around God's actions in relation to his creation, his people, his king and kingdom, his presence (in, for example, the temple or the land), his self-revelation and so on.

Each of these mid-level narratives in turn is included to contribute to the largest theme of what God is doing: bringing himself glory by creating and saving a people for himself through his Son. The big picture is the story of God's salvation and God's Saviour, Jesus Christ. The two questions we need to ask when handling any small-level narrative passage are therefore:

1. How does this fit with and eventually link to what God is doing in Jesus?
2. Having figured that out, how does it therefore apply to us?

Where are we today in this diagram? The answer is: *post-Jesus.*

Be careful not to misunderstand the diagram. Its point is not that we are somehow more important in God's plan than Jesus. It shows that when we're drawing lines of application from Old Testament narratives, we have to go first to Jesus and ask how his coming, life, death and resurrection affect that narrative. Only then can we ask: "what does it means for people in Jesus, for the recipients of his new covenant?"

If we don't follow this principle of making Jesus the primary way we understand the whole Bible, we will perpetually be tempted to allegorise or moralise. We will put ourselves in the shoes of Bible characters without carefully thinking whether that is an appropriate way to handle the text.

The story of promise

The Bible is the story of God's salvation. Genesis 1 – 3 describes how God made the world good and made humanity to enjoy his world. He placed us under his good rule—a rule that brought life and freedom. But humanity rejected God's rule and incurred God's wrath. The rest of the Bible is the story of how God sets about restoring what was lost and fulfilling his purposes in creation. The agenda for salvation is set out in the promises God made to Abraham:

1. **A people who know God.** "I will make you into a great nation and I will bless you; I will make your name great, and you will be a blessing" (Genesis 12 v 2).
2. **A place of rest.** "The Lord appeared to Abram and said, "To your offspring I will give this land."" (Genesis 12 v 7)
3. **Blessing to the nations.** "I will bless those who bless you, and whoever curses you I will curse; and all peoples on earth will be blessed through you" (Genesis 12 v 3).
4. **A king and a kingdom.** There's one further element which is anticipated in the promise to Abraham (Genesis 17 v 6), but which comes in a new and explicit way in God's covenant with David. God promises that one of David's descendants will always rule God's people (2 Samuel 7 v 11-16). As the kings of Israel failed to lead the people faithfully, the expectation grew of a coming Saviour-King, the Messiah from the line of David, who would rescue God's people.

These promises drive the Bible story. They're affirmed in covenants with Abraham, with Moses, with David, and in the new covenant that Christ makes. A covenant is a formally agreed promise—"a contract" we might say today. There are different covenants, but underlying them is one promise.

> Scripture foresaw that God would justify the Gentiles by faith, and announced the gospel in advance to Abraham: "All nations will be blessed through you." **Galatians 3 v 8**

Paul says that the promise to Abraham is the gospel announced in advance. The promise that was made to Abraham is the same promise that comes to us in the gospel.

The Bible is the story of how God fulfils this promise to Abraham. The Old Testament is the story of how God partially fulfils the promise in the life of Israel. But each partial fulfilment points to its ultimate fulfilment through Jesus. And along the way the promise gets bigger because God's ultimate purposes are for a new humanity in a new creation. The promise is fulfilled *through* Jesus and *in* the new creation.

- So the Old Testament is about God and the story of how he fulfils his promise to send a Saviour King who will create a new people in a new land (Luke 24 v 25-27).
- But the Old Testament also contains stories that are meant to be examples and warnings to us (1 Corinthians 10 v 6, 11; Hebrews 3 v 7 v 7 – 4 v 11; 11 v 1-40).

The key to applying the Old Testament is to see the connection between these two statements. The examples are examples to us of faith (or warnings of a lack of faith) in the promises and provision of God. That's the point the writer of Hebrews makes in Hebrews 4 and 11. The heroes of Hebrews 11 did what they did because of faith. The generation that didn't enter the land disobeyed God "because of their unbelief" (3 v 19). The writer draws a connection between their faith (or lack of faith) in God's promise and our faith in the gospel. So his application is:

> Therefore, since the promise of entering his rest still stands, let us be careful that none of you be found to have fallen short of it. For we also have had the good news proclaimed to us, just as they did; but the message they heard was of no value to them, because they did not share the faith of those who obeyed. **Hebrews 4 v 1-2**

In Genesis 16 Abraham was wrong to sleep with Hagar not so much because it was immoral (which it was), but because it betrayed a lack of faith in God's promise. Abraham was taking things into his own hands instead of trusting God to fulfil his promises. And that's what we often do when, for example, we try to establish our identity instead of resting in Christ, or when we manipulate people rather than trusting God's purposes.

So the story of David and Goliath is primarily an illustration of how God's anointed King rescues God's people. David is the christ (the word "*christ*" means "*the anointed One*"). As such, he is a pointer to *the* Christ, Jesus, the Son of David, who conquers death on behalf of God's people. But the story also shows what we can achieve if we believe in God's promise to protect his people. We can attempt great things for God because "the battle is the LORD's" (1 Samuel 17 v 47).

Ideas for action

Four key promises

The Old Testament is the story of God's unfolding promise of salvation, which is fulfilled in Christ. God promises:

1. A people who know God.
2. A place of rest.
3. Blessing to the nations.
4. A king and a kingdom.

As we read the Old Testament we can look to see how God is partially fulfilling each strand of his promises in the story of Israel:

- The partial *fulfilments* of the promise illustrate the ultimate fulfilment in Christ.
- The *partial* nature of their fulfilment points to the need for Christ fully to fulfil God's promises.

So as you read a passage of the Bible, ask yourself the following questions:

- What's happening to each element of the promise at this point in the story?
- What does this story tell us about God and his rule?
- How does it contrast with, point to or illuminate the work of Christ?
- How does it give us confidence in the word of promise that comes to us in the gospel?
- What does it tell us about how people are to respond to and apply the word of promise in our lives today?

Four key questions

When preaching any passage of Scripture, especially Old Testament passages, ask yourself the following four questions:

- What aspects of the character of God does the passage reveal, and how does Christ exemplify this?
- What aspects of the identity of humanity does the passage reveal, and how does Christ fulfil this?
- What aspects of the promises of God does the passage reveal, and how does Christ complete this?
- What aspects of the need of humanity does the passage reveal, and how does Christ meet this?

9 PREACHING TO UNBELIEVERS

Principle

Because our problem is the heart, your sermons should address the heart.

Consider this

David Watson, a British evangelical leader of an earlier generation said:

> In sweeping contrast to the dithering caution of most academic theologians, who were efficiently undermining the faith of some of my friends, Billy Graham led a mission to [Cambridge] University in November 1955. Interestingly, when he tried, somewhat unsuccessfully, to be academic, his preaching lacked power. But when he accepted the apparent foolishness of the message of "Christ crucified" and preached it with simplicity and integrity, the power of God's Spirit was manifestly at work, changing the lives of many undergraduates. It was a lesson I have never forgotten.[1]

1 Cited in Timothy Dudley-Smith, *John Stott: The Making of a Leader,* IVP, 1999, 364-365.

Bible background

Read 1 Corinthians 1 v 18-31

- What counters the wisdom and power of the world?
- How are people saved?

Read 1 Corinthians 2 v 1-5

- How does Paul preach to unbelievers?
- How does Paul not preach to unbelievers?
- What's the content of his message?

Read all about it

Romans 1 says: "what may be known about God is plain" (1 v 19), but people "suppress the truth by their wickedness" (1 v 18). The fool who "says in his heart, 'There is no God'" is not intellectually deficient. The problem is "they are corrupt" and "their deeds are vile" (Psalm 14 v 1).

In other words, it's not that people *cannot* believe, but that they *will not* believe. We will not believe in God because we don't want to live with God. "For although they knew God," continues Romans 1, "they neither glorified him as God nor gave thanks to him." As a result "their thinking became futile and their foolish hearts were darkened" (1 v 21). In other words, our thinking becomes twisted because we're readily finding reasons to justify the life we want to live.

Preach to the heart

This has big implications for preaching to unbelievers. It means our job is not simply to convince them that the truth is true, but also that the truth is good. We need to make people wish it were true before they'll really engage with whether it is true. So our goal (as it is with believers) is not simply to capture their minds, but to capture their affections for Christ. We need to portray the grace and glory of God in a compelling and attractive way—because it really is compelling and attractive!

The "God" assumed in western thought is either a solitary, powerful being who demands our obedience, or a cosy "Father Christmas" or "Sky Fairy" figure whose job is to do nice things for us. That is the kind of "God" most people believe in, if they have any notion of God at all. They're also the kind of "Gods" most atheists and agnostics have (rightly) rejected. But they aren't the God of the Bible. The true God is a Trinity of persons eternally existing in love.

The Father so delights in his Son and the Son *so* delights in the Father through the Spirit, that the triune God created the whole of creation to share their mutual delight. The Trinity extends its life of love to humanity. The gospel is not simply that Jesus died in our place so our sins can be forgiven. It is that, but so much more. Stopping with a message of sins forgiven portrays God merely as a judge.

It's only half the gospel. Who wants to love a judge? Who would feel drawn to such a God? The gospel is that the Father sent the Son so we can be adopted as his children, and he sent the Spirit of his Son so we can know ourselves to be adopted as his children. That's the invitation of the gospel, an invitation to share the Trinity's life of love.

Preach Jesus

A perpetual temptation for preachers is to provide philosophical answers to intellectual questions. But we're called to preach "Christ and him crucified". By all means, take people's questions seriously and address their intellectual concerns. But ensure that delighting in Jesus is central. Your hearers need to know you are captivated not by some fascinating matter of philosophy or some troubling issue in the world or our lives, but by him. Make something he said or something he did the focus for your response. We don't counter the wisdom of this world with our own wisdom. It's "Christ Jesus, who has become for us wisdom from God—that is, our righteousness, holiness and redemption" (1 Corinthians 1 v 30). So our boast is in him.

Suppose we're dealing with the issue of miracles. We might begin by empathising with people, by admitting that miracles appear weird to us. We want to engage seriously with people's intellectual questions. So we might show how science and religion are not in opposition or how miracles are possible if God exists. We might explore the evidence for the resurrection on the basis that this the miracle upon which Christianity stands or falls.

But we also want to show how people's attitude to miracles is shaped by their presuppositions (since science can neither prove nor disprove miracles because, by definition, miracles are outside the normal cause and effect studied by science). If you love God, then you won't have a problem believing in miracles. If you hate the idea of God, then you'll readily find reasons to reject his existence.

We'll also want to paint the attractions of the gospel. We might suggest it's not surprising we find miracles weird because they don't belong in our world since they're actually pointers to the *coming world* anticipated in the resurrection. Or you might say that the resurrection means Jesus is alive and we can know God.

Preach with patience

A generation or two ago most people in the west had a basic understanding of Christianity. To preach evangelistically was to proclaim God's grace in Christ and exhort people to faith and repentance. There are some situations in which this approach is still relevant. But in many contexts this shared understanding has been replaced by a deep indifference towards, or suspicion of, Christianity.

Think of people on a spectrum from zero, which is actively hostile to the gospel, to ten, which is people saying: "What must I do to be saved?" Most people in the west are towards the bottom end of this notional spectrum. And we can't expect to bring them from zero to ten in one go. Most of the time there are just too many ideas for them to take on board. If we can simply nudge people along the spectrum a couple of steps, then that is success. God is sovereign in salvation and we can trust him to fulfil his purposes in people's lives.

So at evangelistic events like carol services, our normal approach is often simply to try to tease our hearers. We are inviting people to begin a process of exploration. So we aren't attempting to explain everything. Jesus, it seems, often used this strategy. He didn't just hand people answers. He made them think for themselves. Too often in our preaching we take the playful approach of Jesus and flatten it out into three clear principles. As a result people are not drawn into the story or left thinking how they would respond. The word doesn't get under their radars. They're able to reject it before it can begin to subvert their thinking.

We can be playful, undermining their assumption and enticing their interest. We can use words like "suppose", "perhaps", "maybe" and "if". "Suppose for a moment there is a God. Is it possible he wants a relationship with you?" "If Jesus *did* rise from the dead then perhaps his claims are true." We're inviting them into a dialogue, a process of thought, as they think through the implications for themselves.

Preach for a response

But remember there are also people at eight and nine on our spectrum. It's not culturally acceptable to tell people they're wrong and need to change. But, as Paul says: "If I were still trying to please people, I would not be a servant of Christ" (Galatians 1 v 10). People need to be called to faith and repentance. We're preaching for a response. The gospel is not an option for people to consider. Jesus has been given all authority and sends us to proclaim his kingship and call people to obedience (Matthew 28 v 18-20).

The evangelistic "pitch" of Jesus was a call to die: "Whoever wants to be my disciple must deny themselves and take up their cross and follow me" (Mark 8 v 34). Anyone who accepts this call has a lot of other discipleship issues already sorted out, at least in principle! If you downplay this call at the beginning (perhaps because you feel the need for results), then you create problems further along the line.

It's striking how specific the call to faith and repentance often was in the ministry of Jesus. Few of us would answer the question: "What must I do to inherit eternal life?" with a call to sell your possessions and give the money to the poor. But this is what Jesus says to the rich man in Mark 10 v 17-22. Jesus recognises the man's need to choose whether God or money will rule his heart. We don't just call people to repent of idolatry in general, but to repent of their specific idols.

Turning from sin in repentance and turning to God in faith go together. If they're separated, then repentance can become a work we perform to earn God's approval. We're not simply calling people to stop doing bad things. We're inviting them to embrace the One who is bigger and better than anything sin offers. The call to repentance is itself good news. It's not that we have to give up something we enjoy in exchange for the promise of heaven. We're being invited to the true joy of knowing the triune God of love.

We're also called, not only to repent of our sinful actions, but also to repent of our good works. As Tim Keller points out, many people assume Christianity is about earning God's approval. We need to address this before religious people can truly receive Christ, because otherwise a call to repentance is heard as a call to moral reform. People need to repent of their good works done for the wrong reasons. But non-religious people also need to hear you deconstructing religion because they, too, assume that this is what Christianity is.

How do we do this? We identify the sin underneath the sin. In other words, behind wrong behaviour are wrong beliefs and desires. We put other things in the place of God. Our underlying sin always involves a failure to believe the gospel. Addressing this enables you to speak the gospel afresh to Christians and non-Christians.

Sex outside of marriage, for example, is a sin. But it's also the symptom of a deeper sin: the attempt to find identity or fulfilment apart from Christ. To a woman who'd had five husbands Jesus said:

> Everyone who drinks this water will be thirsty again, but whoever drinks the water I give them will never thirst. Indeed, the water I give them will become in them a spring of water welling up to eternal life.
>
> **John 4 v 13-14**

It is critical that we are up-front about the life that Jesus Christ is offering when calling people to follow Christ. The danger is that they assume that the good news is just about getting their sins forgiven. While this is gloriously true, both authors have met people who think that's all there is to it. Nobody ever told them that they aren't just forgiven because of Jesus' death, but also now included in his life, his purposes, his mission and his disciple-making team. They have embraced passivity because nobody ever told them otherwise. If we let people become Christians with this incomplete message, then before long they will be passengers and consumers of religion rather than passionate disciples.

Questions for reflection

- Imagine you've been given the sermon title, "How can a loving God allow suffering?" How might you preach to the heart? How might you preach Jesus?

- What are the main prejudices people have about Christianity in your ministry context? How might you address these in a way that offers good news?

PART FOUR

THE PRIORITIES OF PREACHING

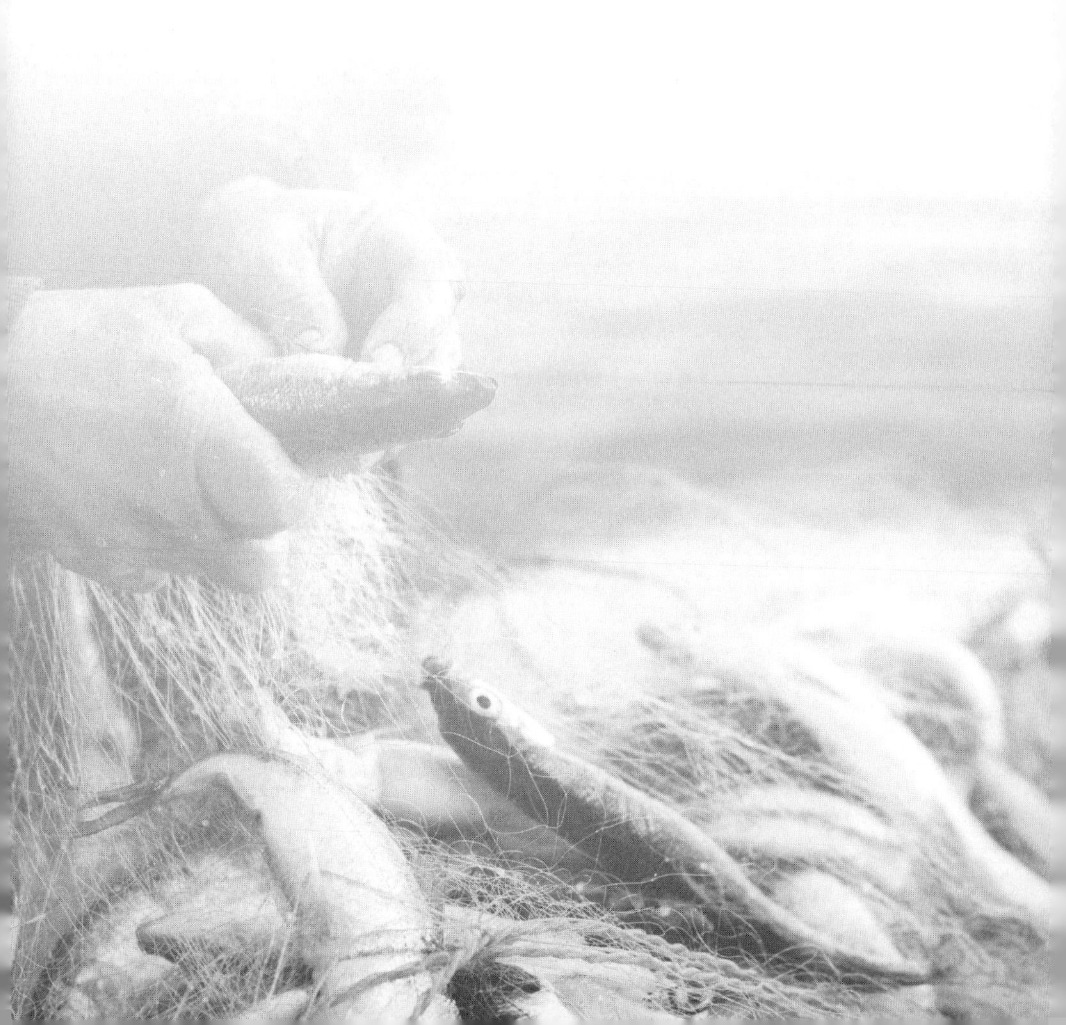

10 MAKE IT CLEAR

Principle

Your sermon should make the passage clear.

Consider this

Dave had asked Brian to give him some feedback on his sermon. "I'm trying really hard to be faithful to the text," he'd said. "But my sermons never seem very exciting. Does that matter?"

So Brian listened carefully as Dave taught from Paul's letter to the Romans. He read the first verse. He explained what all the key words meant. He pointed to some other verses that also used those words. And then he made an application to similar situations in our lives. Then he moved on to the next verse. Same procedure. Eight verses later he was done.

"Any feedback?" Dave asked later.

"You didn't really explain the message of the passage," replied Brian.

"What do you mean?" said Dave defensively. "I went through it verse by verse."

Brian thought for moment.

What should he say?

Bible background
Read Acts 8 v 26-39

- Why did God send Philip to the Gaza road? What did the eunuch need?
- What questions is the eunuch asking?
- What does Philip preach?
- What's the outcome?

Read all about it

There are three key components to a good sermon: accuracy, application and adoration. They can be expressed in three simple exhortations to:

- make it clear
- make it real
- make it felt

We need to make the text of scripture *clear* because it is the word of God. But we also need to make it *real* because we want people not only to be hearers of the word, but doers of the word. We want people to see how the word connects with their lives and how they can live that word. But our aim is affections won for Christ. We want people to be filled with praise for God. So we also need to make the text *felt*. We need to portray Christ in all his beauty so that the glory of God is seen and felt in people's hearts. In the final analysis, the goal of all preaching is worshipping hearts being transformed by the wonder of God.

The process begins with working on the text so its message is clear to us.

Authors, texts and readers

The meaning of a passage is the meaning intended by the *authors*—both the human author and the divine Author (though Old Testament writers did not always fully appreciate how what they wrote would be fulfilled). This meaning is conveyed by the text of the Bible. So our job is to identify the meaning intended by the authors by playing close attention to the *text*.

But *readers* come with their own assumptions and prejudices. We need to be careful not to let these distort our reading of the Bible. Proverbs 1 v 7 says: "The fear of the LORD is the beginning of knowledge, but fools despise wisdom and instruction". Knowledge is more than facts. It's a relationship with the One who is the Truth. People reject the truth about God because they don't want to submit to him. So we need to read the Bible humbly and obediently, praying for the Spirit to open our eyes. And we need to read it with other Christians so they can challenge our distorted understandings and challenge us to live in obedience to the truth.

The wood and the trees

The saying: "You can't see the wood for the trees" can be true of understanding the Bible. It's very easy to get so involved in the detail (individual trees) that you miss the overall message of a passage or book (the wood). The Bible is not a series of isolated statements of principle. The stories are stories with tensions and resolutions. The letters are sustained arguments. Only the book of Proverbs comes close to being isolated sayings. So we need to understand individual verses. But our aim is always to understand what the author is saying in paragraphs, stories and books as a whole.

This means that understanding the Bible involves constantly

moving to and fro between the details and the big picture. The more you understand the detail of individual verses, the more you'll understand the big picture of whole passages and Bible books. And the more you understand the big picture, the more you'll understand the detail.

So when you're starting to explore a book of the Bible, read the book two or three times, asking questions like these:

- To whom is it addressed?
- What are their issues, questions, challenges or threats?
- If it were a conversation, what would be going on at the other end?
- How does the author respond?

Then have a first go at summarising the overall message of the book.

Here are some key questions to apply to individual passages. Although they're roughly in order, in practice you will move backwards and forwards between them. Working on a passage is rarely a clear step-by-step process. It's a more creative process than that.

1. What does the passage say?

- Put it in your own words, looking up words you don't understand.
- What's the argument or flow of the passage?
- How does each sentence and paragraph fit into the flow of the passage?
- Are there repeated words or phrases, or parallel statements?
- What's the historical and cultural background of the passage?
- Does this help us understand what is being said?
- Are the geographical references relevant?
- The meaning of names can be significant especially when naming is part of the story.

2. Why does the author say it in this way?

- Why has the author chosen these phrases and arguments, and not others?
- What type of literature is the passage? Is it prophecy, poetry, history, wisdom, a letter or a parable? How does this affect how we read the passage?
- What imagery or hyperbole is used?
- With stories, are there any editorial comments?
- What's the writer's perspective on the story?
- Are there any surprises—something the author has said that we wouldn't expect? How can we account for these surprises?

3. Why does the author say it here?

- Who's being addressed in this passage? (There can be two audiences: parables, for example, are addressed to Jesus' hearers and to the readers of the Gospels.)
- How does the passage address their needs?
- How does this passage fit into its immediate context?
- What's the flow of the argument?
- What's the overall message of the book?
- What does this passage contribute to the message of the book? How does the overall message of the book inform this passage?
- Why do this passage and book belong at this point in the Bible's story?
- How does this passage relate to the Bible's overall story?
- How does it point to Christ?
- How do we see the core promises of God (a people who know God, a place of rest, blessing to the nations, a king and a kingdom) being partially or fully fulfilled?
- What does it show us about the gospel?
- Does the Bible refer to the passage anywhere else? In the case of an Old Testament passage, how is it used in the New Testament? In the case of a New Testament passage, does it

allude to Old Testament passages and, if so, how does their background inform our understanding of the New Testament passage?
- What else does the Bible say about this theme?

The key questions in this stage of the process are **What? How?** and **Why?** But having worked out what the main ideas in the passage are, there is a crucial next question to ask: **"So what?"** or **"How does this apply today?"** That's the question we'll turn to in the next chapter.

Questions for reflection

- Take a passage that you're preaching on soon and ask the What? How? Why? questions listed above.

Ideas for action

You don't have to work on a passage on your own. You could create a "teachers group" involving current and potential preachers in your church. Meet for an hour to explore together the passage that will be taught a week or two later. This will help to model good ways to understand and interpret the Bible (hermeneutics) as well as providing a fruitful way of engaging with the text.

11 MAKE IT REAL

Principle

Your sermon should make the passage real.

Consider this

Doug was preaching on the sovereignty of God next Sunday. He'd chosen his text and done his exegesis. He felt that he had some good material. But now he had to work out how to apply it.

The sovereignty of God was such a big subject, a lofty subject. It seemed far removed from the experience of his congregation. On Wednesday night he lay in bed worrying about it. He was tired the next morning. A traffic jam on the way to the office made him even more irritable. "What am I going to do?" he kept asking himself.

Then on Friday a crisis blew up and there was no time to work on his sermon. He was supposed to be giving pastoral counsel, but he kept worrying about his sermon. His week was going from bad to worse. He wondered about spending Saturday on the sermon, but he knew the children had been looking forward to a day out. By now his anxiety levels were at maximum. Why was this happening to him? If only he could crack it.

How was he going to apply the sovereignty of God to people's lives if he couldn't apply it to his own? Should he dare to tell the congregation that he had struggled and failed to apply it to his own life this week? After all, what would people think of him as a leader and preacher?

Bible background
Read Philippians 1 v 9-11

- Identify the causal connections in this prayer. What leads to what?
- Why does Paul want Christians to grow love that is full of knowledge and insight?
- What's the end goal?
- What does this mean for our preaching?

Read all about it

The Bible is a contemporary word. Hebrews introduces a quote from Psalm 95 with the words, "So, as the Holy Spirit says: "Today, if you hear his voice…" (3 v 7). The words of Psalm 95 speak "today". And notice that it says: "the Holy Spirit *says*" (present tense). The Spirit not only spoke long ago. The Spirit speaks today.

The job of preaching is not to *make* the word contemporary. It already is contemporary. Trying to make the word contemporary actually involves moving *away* from the word to today's world, rather than connecting the two. Our job is to *show* its contemporary relevance—to make it real for our hearers. Application is not something we *impose* on the text. Good applications are really "implications" that *arise from within the text.*

Connect the word to the world

We want people to feel that this is a contemporary word for them. Even if they don't like what they hear, it should sound contemporary. Indeed, until it sounds contemporary, they'll probably not object to the challenge of the gospel. What people thought in the past is at best mildly interesting. It's God word *today* that challenges people's lives.

If your sermon presents an answer to a difficult question or a pastoral concern, then take time to outline the issue with genuine understanding and sensitivity. Your aim should be for people to realise that you're describing their feelings or struggles. Don't gloss over this so you can get to the "meat" of your sermon. If you're glib, then people will assume that your message is superficial.

It's important to empathise with the congregation. Life is hard. Following Jesus Christ can be hard. People in our churches have real issues, real sufferings and real temptations. They really want to know how to do what God says in the Bible this week. Sometimes they worry that the word of God sounds weird or socially unacceptable, and wonder how they can ever follow it or tell it to their friends. If you never acknowledge this, then your hearers will wonder what planet you're on. But if you spend time describing a problem, then when you bring the word to bear on that issue, it comes with real power.

Try to hear your sermons as a newcomer would hear them. Don't assume that people know their Bibles well. Avoid jargon. Try to anticipate how people will respond to the word.

- *Acknowledge cultural distance.* You might say: "I know this seems strange to us, but..." People may be thinking: "This is just weird". It's important to acknowledge this and then provide explanations. You might say: "This was common in the culture of the time. I guess an equivalent today might be..."
- *Acknowledge doubt.* You might say: "I know this is hard to believe, but..." Anticipate objections. If you don't address them, then your hearers are unlikely to engage with what you go on to say.
- *Acknowledge suffering.* Remember there'll be people in your congregation who are struggling. There's a place for a theoretical explanation of suffering, but recognise that some of hearers may need pastoral consolation. Recognise where your message is challenging. Anticipate those who'll find your application hard, and acknowledge their fears or problems.

You won't always have time comprehensively to address doubts or struggles. But acknowledging them will go a long way in preventing people switching off because they've decided this is not for them.

Another helpful way of making connections is to link the Bible story to people's stories or the stories of the culture, something Jesus did all the time.

- **Our identity = creation.** *How do people understand who they are and what they are meant to be?*
- **Our problem = the fall.** *What do they think is wrong with them and the world, or who do they blame?*
- **Our solution = redemption.** *What do they think needs to happen for things to be put right?*
- **Our hopes = consummation.** *What are they hoping will give them meaning, satisfaction or fulfilment?*

Every time the Bible speaks of creation, fall, redemption or consummation, it is an opportunity either to affirm or confront people's understanding of their identity, problem, solution or hopes.

Finally, you'll naturally develop your sermon as a dialogue with those around as you prepare. If you spend all week in commentaries, then your sermon will feel like a conversation with scholars. If you spend time with your church or in your neighbourhood, then your sermon will more naturally communicate with your hearers.

And don't just preach to the people who are there. Try to preach to those you'd *like* to be there. Christians will only invite their friends if they're confident it'll be relevant.

Apply the word to the world

> Do not merely listen to the word, and so deceive yourselves. Do what it says. **James 1 v 22**

As we've seen, the goal of preaching is that God might be glorified as lives are changed through hearts won for Christ. The goal is action—action that glorifies God. This means application is not an add-on at the end of a sermon. Application is the point. No passage of Scripture was written just to provide information about God.

This doesn't mean you can't preach a sermon the aim of which is to present God to people's hearts so they're blown away by his goodness or glory or grace. But in that case, getting people staggered by the glory of God *is* the application.

1. What were the implications to the people to whom it was originally written?

To identify the application today, first identify the application to the original readers.

- What response did the author want from his hearers or readers?
- To whom was the author writing and why? (Remember there can be two audiences: hearers and readers.)
- Why does the author tell them what he does?
- What does he want them (1) to think, (2) to feel and (3) to do?
- What is the *power* of the passage? In other words, *how* does it expect to accomplish the things it addresses?

Understanding why the author said it *then* enables you to work out what it says for us *now*. Your main application should reflect the main points of the passage, not tangential points, unless you have a really strong reason for focussing on a subsidiary theme.

2. What are the implications now?

Try to focus on the implications that are specifically relevant to your congregation. You're not trying to create a model sermon on this passage that could be preached anywhere. Indeed, one of the dangers of putting sermons on the internet is that preachers try to deliver universal sermons. Your aim is to show how God's word speaks today to the specific group of people in front of you.

Don't just go after individual application. Much of the Old Testament was written to God's people as a community and most of the New Testament was written to local congregations. And God's word doesn't speak to a Christian ghetto. It's a public word for the world.

Addressing missional implications will also help your congregation share God's gospel with their unbelieving friends and apply it to their work, politics, cultural engagement and so on. So ask yourself:

- What are the **personal** implications (for individuals within the congregation)?
- What are the **communal** implications (for the congregation as a whole)?
- What are the **missional** implications (for people in our neighbourhood)?

Be sensitive to the spiritual condition of your hearers. One of the continual challenges for preachers is preaching to congregations with people in a mix of spiritual conditions. It's important to handle these carefully and sometimes make distinctions otherwise:

- the sensitive people who need comfort will be challenged by what you say to the complacent
- the complacent people who need challenge will be comforted by what you say to the sensitive

Good application requires not only a good understanding of the word, but a good understanding of people. If you think of sermon preparation as a process that takes place in a study surrounded by books, then you'll *never* make it real. We need to know our people—the Christians in our congregation, and the unbelievers we're trying to reach. Some preachers really should get out more!

Finally you should ask yourself, both as you prepare and afterwards:

- will this message draw faith from the hearts of my hearers?
- will they want to be unashamed worshippers of God, casting themselves on him as their king as a result of this sermon

- will people want to do what the passage requires as a result of this sermon?

If the answer to any of these is "no", then it isn't yet as helpful a message as it can be.

Questions for reflection

Take a passage that you're preaching on soon and ask: **so what? What response did the author want?** Ask yourself:

- What are the **personal** implications (for individuals within the congregation)?

- What are the **communal** implications (for the congregation as a whole)?

- What are the **missional** implications (for people in our neighbourhood)?

Ideas for action

There are more ways of telling people what they should do than simply telling them what they should do!

Case studies

Apply the passage to a fictional or semi-fictional case study. People are much better at transferring application from one specific situation to their own situation than they are at applying abstract principles. You could introduce the scenario(s) in the introduction to your sermon and then return to them in your conclusion.

Commendation

You don't have to apply a passage by telling people what they're not doing. You can also commend people for what they are doing. Just think how often Paul commends his hearers in his letters. And think how this impacts a congregation: those who are doing it are motivated to continue, while those who aren't doing it want to be included in the future commendation.

Instant application

It may be that there is an application that is communal or missional that you realise you are not providing an opportunity for as a church. It may be right for you to lead the way in repentance with this, and call for others to follow. Or at least ask for people to be part of a team that thinks through how you as a church can be obedient to the call of the God in this area.

12 MAKE IT FELT

Principle

Your sermon should make the passage felt.

Consider this

Their pastor had preached on the announcement by Jesus that Jerusalem would be destroyed. It was a tricky passage and he'd done a great job in explaining it in its historical context.

Then he'd shown them that Jerusalem's judgment was a pointer to the judgment of all humanity. When they'd first read the passage, Dave had wondered what to make of it. But now he felt he understood what was going on. Yet something didn't feel right.

They had closed with a rousing hymn and now Charlie was standing talking to him about his holiday plans.

Something was missing—*but what?*

Bible background

Read Matthew 13 v 44

- What's the motivation of the man in the story?
- What's the treasure?

Read Philippians 1 v 25-26

- What's the goal of Paul's ministry?

Read Philippians 3 v 7-11

- What's Paul's treasure?
- What kind of a life does it produce?

Read all about it

So far, as you've prepared your sermon you've worked hard to present its meaning ("make it clear") and its implications ("make it real"). But your job is not yet done.

If that's all you do, then you'll have presented a good lecture on the passage. But, as we saw in part one, our aim is not simply education. Our aim is to capture people's affections for Christ. The process of capturing people's affections must build on the foundation of presenting the meaning and implications of the passage clearly. But it must be more than that. We need to think about *how* we communicate. We need to make the passage *felt*.

Think for a moment about how the Bible communicates its message. It includes gripping stories, pithy sayings, stirring speeches, stark warnings, enacted parables, vivid imagery. Again and again it gets under your skin. It's full of colour, texture and life. It's not a series of lectures. Perhaps the closest approximation to lectures are the New Testament letters, but in fact they too are full of personal touches and impassioned appeals. Above all, the Bible gives us gospel motives for our actions. This is much more than merely looking for an emotional response. That would only produce a temporary change. Our aim is to capture people's affections.

If you just preach to minds and wills, then you'll preach legalism. Your message will be: "This is what you should do". And that, by itself without qualification, is legalism. We must also preach to the heart. We must speak of gospel motives.

How was it felt then?

So go back to the passage one more time. How did the original author make it felt?

- How does the passage use language, imagery and suspense to convey its message?
- What motives for change does the passage present?
- How does the passage connect application (the imperatives of the gospel) with the truth of who we are in Christ (the indicatives of the gospel)?
- How does what we should do flow out of what Christ has done?
- What in the passage would have been surprising or shocking for the first hearers or readers?

Consider the genre of Scripture. If you've been preaching for any length of time, you will have become used to considering the way genre affects the meaning of a passage. But genre should also affect the way we *preach* the passage.

Consider how you might preach narrative through stories, poetry poetically, prophecy prophetically and wisdom wisely. Consider the stories of the Bible. If God had simply wanted us to draw three axioms from them, then he'd have given us three axioms instead of a story. The Bible is full of stories because stories draw us in and get under our radar. They shape our values and priorities, often without us realising it.

How is it felt now?

Worship over the text. Pray through the passage. As we've said already, work on the passage until it moves you. Then make it your aim to move your hearers in the same way.

Let your words reflect the wonder of the passage. Don't talk about glorious things without being excited. Look for interesting, gripping phrases. Otherwise you will say one thing with your mouth, but deny it with your demeanour.

C. S. Lewis famously gave this advice on writing:

> Don't use adjectives which merely tell us how you *want* us to feel about the thing you are describing. I mean, instead of telling us a thing was "terrible," describe it so that we'll be terrified. Don't say it was "delightful"; make *us* say "delightful" when we've read the description. You see, all those words (horrifying, wonderful, hideous, exquisite) are only like saying to your readers, "Please will you do my job for me."[1]

The same principle applies to preaching. The more a preacher tells me how I should feel about something, the more I'm inclined to suspect he hasn't done his job well. So don't tell people how they should feel about the truth in your passage. Instead, expound that truth so the truth evokes those feelings in them. Describe what God is doing in the passage in such a way that the beauty, glory and majesty of God shine out. At least make that your aim, even if you can't pull it off every time!

1 C. S. Lewis, *Letters to Children*, Scribner, 1996, 64.

A good way of making the message felt is to use a repeated phrase throughout the sermon or at the conclusion of a series of scenarios.

Look for the point at which the passage subverts our thinking. Look for the point where the knife, as it were, is twisted. How was the passage shocking and surprising to its first readers? What's the shock or surprise today? How might I recreate that moment in my preaching?

Use direct questions, as if you expect people to speak back to you. "Who knows what happens next?" "How many of us have done this recently?" "You know this is true in your life, don't you?" Provide tests for self-examination. "Maybe we don't think of ourselves as a Pharisee, but have we ever looked down on someone else?" To create immediacy, use the present tense if you're retelling a story. "Jesus goes to the temple and says ..." rather than "Jesus went to the temple and said..."

John Stott says the goal of a sermon is to "storm the citadel of the will and capture it for Jesus Christ". He suggests a variety of methods to do this:[1]

- *argument* (anticipate and refute objections)
- *admonition* (warn of the consequences of disobedience)
- *indirect conviction* (arouse moral indignation and then turn it on them as Nathan did with David)
- *pleading* (apply the gentle pressure of God's love)
- *vision* (paint a picture of what is possible through obedience to God in this area)

Exhort people

Don't miss the opportunity to urge people to live as the passage demands. Preachers are more than people who teach and explain. We're heralds, proclaimers, witnesses.

One of the most powerful preachers in my life was actually quite poor at expounding the Bible. But at the end of every sermon he would plead with people to turn to Christ. If he could have gone on

---

1 Condensed from John R. W. Stott, *Between Two Worlds*, 211-216.

his knees without disappearing behind the lectern, then I'm sure he'd have done so. His ministry was powerfully used in the lives of many people.

Paul tells Titus to: "Encourage and rebuke with all authority" (Titus 2 v 15). Ensure your preaching includes both comfort and challenge. Tim Keller says: "Be as affectionate as you are forceful; but as forceful as you are affectionate."[1]

Sometimes it will be good to finish preaching with a prayer along these lines:

> Father, I pray that no one within the sound of my voice will be unreceptive to what you are saying in the Bible. I pray that you will break our hearts. Lead us in your ways. Show us specific ways to live this out this week."

There is one qualification to this: don't pastorally challenge individuals from the pulpit. In other words, if an individual needs challenging then meet with them one-to-one. Don't take the coward's way out and do it through a general challenge as you preach.

If we get to the end of the message and what we've done is explain the underlying propositions of the passage only, then we won't have driven people to consider radical discipleship, putting God's purposes before comfort, life change as they are impacted by the Holy Spirit and really pursuing God in their lives. We might have given a great expository lecture but we will have fallen into the trap of confusing teaching with learning.

The point of the sermon is not that we have delivered truth truly, but that it is truly received, pondered and obeyed. Miss this and your people will think that they are being faithful just because they've heard a message.

1 Tim Keller, *Preaching to the Heart,* audio lectures, Ockenga Institute, 2006.

Questions for reflection

- Take a passage that you are preaching on soon and ask:
  - How did the original author exhort his readers?
  - What motives for change does the passage present?
  - How does the passage move you?
- How can you use words to convey the way the passage makes you feel?
- What changes in conviction, attitude, affections, lifestyle, worship-life and witness would you anticipate if the message of this passage is truly assimilated?
- Review a recent sermon. To what extent did the preacher tell people how to feel? How did they use words to evoke a response to the text?

PART FIVE

THE PROCESS OF PREACHING

13 STRUCTURING A SERMON

Principle

Ensure everything contributes to your main aim.

Consider this

John had had such a good time preparing.

There had been commentaries and references books strewn across his desk, spilling over onto the floor. His Bible software had come up trumps with some fascinating connections. He'd turned the passage into an amazing coloured diagram. He had had so much good material. Surely there was something for everyone. Some interesting cultural observations. Lots of background information. Some application to couples, to parents, to unbelievers, to the workplace. Plenty of cross-references. He was sure it was a feast.

But now Clara was struggling to answer Jane's question. Jane had missed the sermon because she'd been teaching in Sunday school. "Well, Clara, did the sermon rock your world? What was it about?" But Clara was obviously struggling. "It was very interesting," she said kindly. "Oh, go on then, John," said Jane, sensing the embarrassment in the car. "Give me the two-minute version."

John hesitated, unsure how to begin. "I'm not sure a good sermon can be summarised in two minutes."

Bible background
Read Acts 17 v 16-34

- How does Paul introduce his message?
- If Paul had spoken from an outline with headings, what do you think they would be?
- How does he conclude his sermon? Do you think it was concluded for him prematurely?

Read all about it

You've thought about what the text means, how it connects with people today, the implications for your context and the motivations it provides. Now you've got to work out how to turn this big muddle of thoughts into a cohesive and powerful sermon.

The main aim

Start by identifying the main aim of your sermon. You're not simply giving a lecture in which you convey as many ideas from the passage as possible. You're trying to effect change in the hearts and lives of your hearers. If you don't have an aim, then you're unlikely to hit the mark. Often this is called "the big idea" but that can suggest the goal of the sermon is simply teaching people a piece of information. But we want to capture the affections so lives are changed and God is glorified.

The main aim will arise from the key message of the passage *and* the needs of your congregation. So the main aim is not simply a summary of the passage. It's a statement of intent. You need a sense of the impact that you want the passage to have, and how the truth in the passage will create this impact.

This then becomes the organising principle for your material. All your material should be chosen and ordered to achieve this aim.

We don't need to be dogmatic about having just one major idea. There's a danger that we try to squeeze everyone into one mould. That said, the most common mistake of new preachers (and some old ones) is trying to squeeze too much into their sermons. Plenty of sermons fail at this point. By cramming in too much that is tangential to the main aim, they leave people going away with less, not more. Ask yourself if you can remember all the main points from the last sermon you heard or preached. If the answer is "no", then nobody else can either. One point well made, remembered and acted on is frequently better than several unmemorable ones.

Structure

Structure matters. It's easier for someone to follow your preaching if they can tell where you're going! (You, at least, should know where you're going!) People respond better to structure than ramble. But there are three important things to understand about structure:

1. There isn't one correct way to structure a sermon

Normally the structure of a sermon will reflect the structure of the passage. Or you could think of the structure as a stripped-down version of the train of thought that led you to arrive at your main aim. The key question to ask is: *will this be clear, compelling and easy to follow?* Remember that you've done far more work on the passage than your hearers and they don't have the benefit of all your reading.

2. Different genres will create different kinds of sermon

A sermon on an epistle might have headings that present the argument of the passage as a series of logical steps. A sermon on a narrative might retell the story. A sermon on a psalm might begin with a reflection or poem on suffering, perhaps using references in the wider culture. It might then show how these sentiments are echoed in the psalm before showing how the truth in the psalm brings pastoral consolation.

3. The structure of a sermon should reflect the preacher

Preachers have their own personality and style. There are many preachers whom we love to hear who preach in a way we never could. That said, there's real value when you first start preaching in adopting a template. Use some kind of framework to structure your sermons. Over time you'll find yourself departing from the formula. You'll develop your own style and find your own voice. But at the beginning a framework is a great help.

Ideas for action: Three sermon templates

Template #1: state; explain; illustrate; apply

This template is based on John Chapman's *Setting Hearts on Fire*.[1] It's the one that both of us used when we first started preaching. It is a simple outline that will give you better-than-average results fairly quickly. The talk is made up of three parts.

1. The Introduction

2. The Body

- **a. State the point** (what is it that you want to say).
- **b. Show me where you found it in the Bible.**
- **c. Explain it** (tell me what it means).
- **d. Illustrate it** (show me what it is like).
- **e. Apply it** (tell me what to do with it).

Having done this with main point 1, proceed to the next main point and do the same again.

3. The Conclusion

1 John Chapman, *Setting Hearts on Fire*, Matthias Media, 1999, 89-104, p 117-127.

Template #2: plotline to the heart

In an essay entitled "Preaching in a Postmodern City", Tim Keller suggests the following sermon template which starts with application! [1]

1. The plot winds up: What you must do

"This is what you have to do! Here is what the text or narrative tells us that we must do or what we must be."

2. The plot thickens: Why you can't do it

"But you can't do it! Here are all the reasons that you will never become like this just by trying very hard."

3. The plot resolves: How he did it

"But there's One who did. Perfectly. Wholly. Jesus the... He has done this for us in our place."

4. The plot winds down: How, through him, you can do it

"Our failure to do it is due to our functional rejection of what he did. Remembering him frees our heart so we can change like this."

For example, in dealing with the story of David and Bathsheba you might highlight the tyranny and dangers of beauty (body image, pornography, fear of aging). But then via Isaiah 52 and Philippians 2 you might speak of One who gave up glory to become ugly so we could be beautiful in him—a reality that enables us to respond correctly to the tyranny of beauty. We speak first to the mind to create understanding. We then speak to the will and reveal guilt. Finally we speak to the heart to provoke worship.

1 Timothy Keller, *Preaching in a Postmodern City,* The Movement, June 2004.

Template #3: The big picture

Retell the whole Bible story from creation to new creation:

- with a focus on a theme that is prominent in your text.
- with most of your time given to retelling the narrative in your text (slowing down, as it were, when you get to the episode covered in your text)
- with a description of how we're part of this story so we see how it impacts our lives today.

Although this approach can be used with other parts of the Bible, it works especially well for Old Testament narrative. A sermon on Joshua 10, for example, where Joshua defeats five Amorite kings and has his army commanders put their feet on their necks, might unfold like this:

- A long time ago Satan rebelled against God and persuaded humanity to join his rebellion. God could have destroyed humanity but instead he promised that someone who would crush Satan's head. Ever since then, God's people and Satan's people have been engaged in a battle in which Satan has repeatedly tried to wipe out God's people.
- Joshua 10 describes how five kings tried to destroy God's people. But God fought for his people. So God's people can stand with their feet on the necks of their enemies as a sign of God's victory. [This section would be the major part of the sermon with a full retelling of the story, including the historical background and cultural explanations.]
- At the cross Satan tried to wipe out Jesus, the representative of God's people. But Jesus defeated Satan and disarmed his power. As a result you, too, can stand with your feet upon your sin, temptation, fears and bitterness. You can say as Joshua said: "Be strong and courageous, for the Lord is going to do this to all of your enemies."

Questions for reflection

- Listen to a sermon by one of your favourite preachers and analyse its structure. What pattern do they follow? How does the structure help you listen? How does it help the sermon to be memorable?

- Take a passage that you are preaching on soon. What is your main aim? What structure would you naturally choose to preach it? Choose an alternative template from the previous list and use it to develop an outline for your sermon. What are the advantages of using this rather than your own? What are the drawbacks?

- From your own experience so far, compile a list of "top tips" for writing a sermon. There is a list in the "Ideas for action" section of the next chapter, but try to come up with your own before you look at it.

14 WRITING A SERMON

Principle

Let the word do the work.

Consider this

"Try including some illustrations," suggested Pete. He was talking to his assistant pastor.

"But I'm teaching God's word," replied Mark. "I don't need to jazz it up. People ought to listen."

"Yes, I guess so," said Pete. He remembered watching his friend Malcolm drifting off during Mark's sermon. He should have been listening, but he had just finished a night shift.

He thought of young Alex fidgeting at the back, probably not following much of Mark's theological explanations.

He thought of Doreen. He was sure she'd tried to listen, but he also suspected she'd been distracted by her financial concerns.

They all had a responsibility to listen to God's word being preached. True enough.

But what was Mark's responsibility?

Bible background
Read Matthew 5 – 7

Identify the different ways Jesus engages his hearers. Make a list below:

Read all about it

Christians ought to listen to sermons expecting God to speak to them. They ought to be attentive and engaged as they listen.

But preachers can't assume this is happening and we certainly shouldn't take it for granted. **Your job is to make people want to listen,** to get them *engaged* with the word, to help them see the implications for their lives, and to drive home the call to faith and repentance. Prepare as if you have no right to people's attention. Galatians 3 v 1 says: "Before your very eyes Jesus Christ was clearly portrayed as crucified". The words "clearly portrayed" convey the idea of a vivid, verbal portrait of the significance of the cross. It implies more than a mere explanation. The Galatians heard preaching that created a visual picture which captured their imagination.

Let the word do the work

Our principle for this chapter is "let the word do the work". What do we mean by this? Preachers can think they must first determine the meaning of the passage, and then move on to find ways of making the message interesting and relevant. We want to encourage you to let the text do this work for you.

In other words, the text should shape not just the content of your sermon, but its structure, colour, tone and texture. Make your sermon distinctive by using what's distinctive about the text. If you want to drive home a particular point, then drive it home by showing how the text drives it home. Look at the language, repetitions, allusions, illustrations or structural pointers in the text, and use these to give your sermon shape, colour and power.

This means that letting the text do the work actually requires you to do a lot of work on the text! You need to dig deep into what it's saying and how it's saying it. But this work will pay dividends. Not only will your sermon be distinctive, it will be distinctive in a way that mirrors the text of Scripture. If you want to provide a cross-reference, then try doing so using references from the same passage or book. Not only will this give people a stronger sense of the message of the book, it will also avoid your sermons seeming "same-y" as you jump (again) to your favourite verses or applications. In one sense, preachers only ever have one message—the gospel of Christ crucified. But the great variety of Scripture will ensure great variety in our preaching *if* we let the text do the work.

Introductions

Your introduction is your one and only chance to convince the congregation to listen attentively. So you need to grab their attention and persuade them that your message matters. Voice a felt need. Refer to a contemporary issue. Outline a dilemma. Don't start your sermon with an exegetical puzzle. Only scholars and preachers are interested in exegetical puzzles!

A good way to approach your introduction is to think: **if the sermon is the answer, what's the question?** Then use the introduction to state that question in an engaging and provocative way. So, although the introduction is the first thing said, it's normally the last thing you prepare, because you need to be clear the answer is provided by the text before you state the question!

If your sermon is part of a series, you may need to summarise how it fits in the series, especially for the benefit of visitors. On its own, though, this can be a rather flat way to start. It can be better to do this, then pray, and launch into a (hopefully) attention-grabbing introduction after the prayer.

Conclusions

After you've put all your good work on the text into an attractive and engaging form, it's tempting not to give much thought to your conclusion. But this is your chance really to press the point home, to go for goal. So don't bring in new material at this point (unless it's the twist your sermon has been leading up to). Instead, summarise your main ideas (perhaps repeating your headings) and exhort people to respond.

You could finish by re-reading the text (or a key verse in the passage). You could quote an appropriate hymn (especially if you're about to sing it). You could close with a prayer that asks God to effect your main aim (this also allows musicians to get into place if you are going to respond with worship after the message).

If you're preaching evangelistically, then think carefully how you want to conclude. You might invite people to join you as you pray on their behalf. If so, let them know what you're going to pray so they can join in meaningfully. You might invite them to speak to you or someone else afterwards. You might invite them to explore the issues more through an evangelistic course or by reading a Gospel.

Illustrations

Illustrations clarify the truth, bring it to life and show how it connects with people today. They can also give the congregation a helpful break from concentrating on more complex ideas. They can be one line or a story, and they can be real or made up (though don't pass off fictional stories as real ones).

It may sound obvious, but **the point of the illustration is to illustrate!** An illustration is not an aim in itself so it needs to be precisely as long as it needs to be to help people understand what it is enlightening. If people remember the illustration but not the point it was illustrating, then you have things the wrong way round. It might be an entertaining after-dinner speech, but it isn't a good sermon. Your job is not to tell good stories, but preach God's word. If a good story will help, then great. But if it doesn't quite make the point, then save it for another time.

We need to ask of any illustration whether it makes the truth clearer. An illustration will distract people if it's too complicated or you leave loose ends. While you're carrying on with your sermon, people will still be trying to unravel the point of the story or speculating what happened next.

As a general rule, avoid stories which extol your virtues and stories which betray pastoral conversations. Don't go on *ad infinitum* about your particular hobby horses. After a while the fact that you support Arsenal football club will start to turn people off your preaching rather than engage them, if you mention it week after week.

And at all costs don't tell stories at the expense of your family. There are any number of preachers' kids out there who had no defence when dad used them as a preaching tool and who are traumatised by the memory.

Whenever possible, do some work on the text a few weeks before you're going to preach, even if it's only half an hour. This will enable you to meditate on the text over the coming weeks. It also means illustrations and cultural connections may come to you while you're doing other things.

Tone

We need to make people feel we're talking with them. People are all different and we need to preach in the way that enables them to best receive what's being said. We need to pitch what we say at a level which people can understand and receive. If in doubt, be as clear and simple as possible. You don't need to dumb down the content, but you should ensure the language is accessible and people can relate to your illustrations.

I (Marcus) need continual reminders to keep sentences short and not use multiple clauses! Remember, you're not preaching to impress your pastor or whichever preacher's approval you crave. You're serving God by serving the congregation as a whole.

Tragically, it's possible to preach (even preach technically accurately) for *ourselves* rather than for *the glory of God* and the good of the people. Matthew 6 talks about religious leaders ostentatiously parading their religious acts to get applause and approval. Martin Luther summed it up well when he said: "We preach in public for the sake of plain people":

> Cursed be every preacher who aims at lofty topics in the church, looking for his own glory and selfishly desiring to please one individual or another. When I preach here I adapt myself to the circumstances of the common people. I don't look at the doctors and masters, of whom scarcely forty are present, but at the hundred or the thousand young people and children. It's to them that I preach, to them that I devote myself, for they too need to understand. If the others don't want to listen, they can leave ... We preach in public for the sake of plain people. Christ could have taught in a profound way, but he wished to deliver his message with the utmost simplicity in order that common people might understand.[1]

Try to anticipate how people will respond to what you're saying. The word "*sermon*" is a Latin word meaning "*dialogue*" and sermons in the early church often included Q&A. So think of your

1 Martin Luther, *Luther's Works*, Volume 35, American Edition, ed. Jarislav Pelikan and Helmut Lehmann, Fortress Press, 1960, p 235, 383.

sermon as a dialogue with the congregation in which you supply their questions (or, if you are daring, let them voice them!). And ask rhetorical questions back at them: "What would you have done?" "Does that remind you of anything?" "Isn't that how we all think?"

Try to anticipate how people might misunderstand what's being said. In a sermon on love, for example, you might need to deconstruct Hollywood notions of love. New believers will need more explanation. Older believers need to hear the truth in fresh ways. So prepare with your hearers in mind. It's often helpful to think of specific people and imagine the sermon as a conversation with them.

Edit, edit and then edit

We both spend as much time taking material out of our sermons as we do putting it in. Maybe that means we overprepare to start with. But maybe not. Perhaps it's more like boiling down a sauce when you're cooking, boiling off a lot of liquid in order to concentrate and intensify the flavour. We're not giving a lecture so we're not trying to convey as much information as possible. We're trying to intensify the focus on Jesus and capture people's affections for him. So rigorously remove anything that might distract from this. Go through line by line looking at what you can take out. The key test is this: **Does this lead towards the main aim of the sermon?**

Both of us prefer to preach from a full script. We know everyone approaches this differently, but want to commend the idea to you. It's impossible rigorously to go through your message line by line if you don't have a full script, but most people are much more inclined to waffle without one. Telling people that what we're saying from the Bible is true on God's authority is a serious matter. The value of a script is that it allows us to be accountable afterwards for every word that we've said (and gently correct anyone who thinks we said things we didn't). Give it a go. You're likely to find it increases your clarity and the ease with which people can listen to you.

I (Marcus) remember listening to a sermon that contained far too much material. Mid-sermon the person sitting next to me announced loudly: "I've just lost the will to live!" Do everything you can to prevent your hearers reaching this point!

How long?

There's no universal right length for a sermon. It depends on your abilities, your congregation's expectations and the occasion for which you're speaking. But here's a good test: *a sermon should feel as if the preacher has worked to make it shorter by taking out material rather than worked to make it longer by adding material.*

You're not preaching to fill time or impress people with your learning. You're preaching to make an impact. A stick that has been whittled to a point will make more impact than an unworked lump of wood. As French writer Antoine de Saint-Exupery put it:

> You know you have achieved perfection in design, not when you have nothing more to add, but when you have nothing more to take away.

Tim often tells preachers: "There's lots of good material left on the cutting-room floor", an image from the old days of movie-making when movies were shot using physical film. The movie was edited by slicing it up and discarding the unwanted bits, until the floor of the cutting room was covered with discarded pieces. Hours of expensive footage was rejected to produce a two-hour masterpiece.

We need the same process in our sermon preparation. It can be painful. One of the pastors who taught Marcus to preach used to say: "It's like choosing which of your children to shoot!" But producing that 30-minute message with real punch inevitably means that hours of great exegesis and many wonderful insights will be discarded. As Albert Einstein is reputed to have put it:

> Any darn fool can make something complex;
> it takes a genius to make something simple.

Questions for reflection

Think about a sermon you've recently preached or heard. Identify the strengths and weakness of the:

- introduction
- conclusion
- illustrations

Ideas for action

Top tips for sermon-writing

1. Make your main aim shape everything you say.
2. Less (material) is usually more (impact).
3. Make your sermon distinctive by using what's distinctive about the text.
4. Organise your material by using headings.
5. Keep sentences short
6. Use everyday words.
7. Tell stories in the present tense.
8. Anticipate people's questions.
9. Ensure illustrations illustrate the point.
10. Prepare as if you're talking to a specific unbeliever or new believer.
11. Speak your notes aloud.
12. Press home the implications of the message.

Readability and listen-ability

Cut and paste the text of one of your sermons into an online readability checker (like www.read-able.com). This will tell you the reading age required for your prose. But remember people are not reading your sermon. A reading age is not a "listening" age. So the reading age needs to be lower than the age of your listeners. A reading age of 11-12 years old is a good standard for which to aim.

My sermon preparation: *Tim*

I prepare a series as a whole up front. I want to ensure I have the big picture of the book we'll be working through (or a good understanding of the subject if the series is topical). That big picture evolves as the series progresses because the details of each passage finesse your understanding of the book as a whole. But you need some sense of the overall picture before you can begin to make sense of the detail. It's this repeated cycle that makes preaching through a book so exciting.

Four or five weeks before I'm preaching I'll look at the passage for about an hour. The aim is to get the questions, issues and application bubbling around in my mind over the coming weeks.

I do the bulk of the preparation about a week in advance. That's partly because I need to get a draft off to the people who are preparing the meeting and our children's groups.

I leave the final edit to the Sunday morning. I change wording during this edit, but its primary purpose is to *take out* any material that's not absolutely necessary. I leave it until Sunday morning so the material is fresh in my mind when I deliver it a couple of hours later.

My sermon preparation: *Marcus*

I try to give my first attention to the passage at least a week before preaching. It will be far earlier if I am doing a series.

Because meaning almost always follows structure, I start by trying to gain a careful idea of how the flow of thought works in the passage, the surrounding sections and whole book. If I can't describe why this is recorded in this way in this place, then I know I can't yet take the next steps in preparation.

I jot notes down at this stage, spotting where the argument changes and the flow of the passages alters, and what are the connections between sections and ideas. This process frequently leads to some diagrams in which I try to isolate the big themes of the passage, which need to form the big points of the message. I want the balance of my message to follow the balance of the passage.

One thing I find critical to write down is anything that I find surprising, unusual or puzzling, plus anything the original recipients might have found surprising. It's remarkable how often the surprises are the things on which the meaning hangs.

Once I've given the time to answering what the passage meant to its original hearers, I try to give half my preparation and delivery time to the question of how to get under the skin of my hearers. That involves praying.

Then I try to craft the message. I usually do this two days before with a final edit on the day before. I always ask myself how to express the truths of the passage in ways that are most compatible with the passage. I want to find words that do justice to the passage. I search and search for ways of expressing the truths concerned in such a way that people will be affected by them, want to live them out and go away with some idea of how this can be done in the coming week.

And then I see how long it is. If it's too long for the context I am going to preach in, then it's back to the cutting room for more editing.

Questions for reflection

- Given your personality and time pressures, what's a good pattern for your preparation? Write our your ideal below:

15 DELIVERING A SERMON

Principle

Passionate preaching requires a passionate preacher.

Consider this

Jonathan Edwards had poor eyesight and small handwriting. So when he preached, he held his notes close to his face, hiding his face from view. He broke all the rules of good oratory.

His preaching led to revival.

Bible background

Read Acts 20 v 17-38

- How does Paul feel about his message?
- How does Paul feel about the Ephesians?
- How was this reflected in his ministry?

Read all about it

My (Marcus) first experience of regular preaching was in a small church where a dear saint fell asleep within the first two minutes of the sermon every week and snored loudly. We've all had people fall asleep during our sermons. There may be lots of good reasons for this—a sleepless night or medication. But let's ensure our preaching isn't one of them!

Good preachers vary their delivery. They slow down and speed up at different points, raise their voices and lower their voices. Some are good at using their bodies to convey the message and reinforce the points they are making.

The problem is that the more you think about these things, the more unnatural it all becomes. Many young preachers feel timid and suffer from nerves that tend to make them close down their delivery style. Here are some things you can do to help develop your delivery:

- Practise reading your Bible aloud at home to experiment with how to convey meaning through changes of pace and tone.
- Practise your sermons to ensure that you've prepared sound patterns to the words on the page that are natural when spoken aloud—and to ensure you are comfortable with their delivery. This also helps to get the timing right.
- Ensure you look at the congregation when you are preaching. Focus on the people you can see responding with enthusiasm because they will encourage you to preach with enthusiasm.

But in the end, these things arise naturally as an expression of your passion for God and his word. You need to preach with passion rather than adopting some kind of affected emotionalism.

Preach with passion

There's no such thing as dispassionate preaching. It's a contradiction in terms. Dispassionate presentation produces passionless hearers—which is sin. Enthusiasm is catching but so is lack of enthusiasm. Paul describes how for three years he proclaimed the truth in Ephesus "with tears" (Acts 20 v 19, 31). Richard Baxter said: "Though you give the holy things of God the highest praises in words, yet, if you do it coldly, you will seem by your manner to unsay what you said in the matter."[1] Charles Spurgeon wrote:

> If I were asked, "What in a Christian minister is the most essential quality for securing success in winning souls for Christ?" I should reply, "earnestness". And if I were asked a second or a third time, I should not vary the answer. For personal observation drives me to the conclusion that, as a rule, real success is proportionate to the preacher's earnestness.[2]

Jonathan Edwards talked about setting people's affections on the truth, making sure that they were in the direction of the truth revealed and in proportion to it. If he was preaching about joy, then the people should be rejoicing; and if he was preaching about sin, then they should be sorrowing. And so should the preacher and his words. If you preach about joy without words full of joy, then the people won't be joyful. If you preach about sin without words full of horror and shame, then the people won't be seized with the need for repentance.

We all express passion in different ways, but the one thing that isn't acceptable is no passion at all. We cannot preach about Almighty God without thrill, wonder and marvel. It's simply impossible.

How can we preach with passion? You certainly can't fake it. The only effective way to *appear* passionate when you preach is to *be* passionate when you preach! The word needs to impact your heart if you want to impact other people. So pray. Pray through the passage until it moves you. And then pray that it would move your congregation in a similar way.

---

1 Richard Baxter, *The Reformed Pastor*, Banner of Truth, 1974, p 148.

2 Charles H. Spurgeon, *Lectures to My Students*, Zondervan, 1954, p 305.

Preach with conviction

We want our preaching to come with authority. Clearly that comes primarily from the word itself and from the Spirit. But we should preach with conviction. We're not sharing our opinions or our reflections. We're declaring a word from God. Paul says: "Our gospel came to you not simply with words but also with power, with the Holy Spirit and deep conviction" (1 Thessalonians 1 v 5). Peter says: "If anyone speaks, they should do so as one who speaks the very words of God" (1 Peter 4 v 11).

It's normal to feel nervous when you first start preaching. At a practical level, ensure there's some water to hand, as your mouth often dries up when you're nervous. But the key to overcoming nerves is to remember who you are and what you're doing. You're a child of God saved by the grace of God. Your identity doesn't depend on how the next 30 minutes go. Nor does it depend on what others think of you. Only God's opinion really counts and in Christ he delights in you. And what you're about to do is proclaim the word of God in the power of God. Ultimately its effectiveness doesn't depend on your eloquence, but the work of the Holy Spirit.

I (Tim) realised a few years ago that often when I stood up to preach, I thought my sermon was about to be one of the best sermons in the history of the church! Yet when I read through old sermons a few months later, it was agony to think that I'd inflicted this rubbish on my poor congregation.

I decided that this combination of attitudes is actually quite healthy as long as you hold both together. My enthusiasm for my sermon was actually my enthusiasm for the passage. The word of God had gripped me and I was excited about sharing its message with the congregation. That allowed me to preach with conviction. But remembering my retrospective assessment of my sermons would prevent me from growing proud!

Using notes

Write out your talk as you would speak it and not as you would write it. Use short sentences. Replace commas with separate sentences. Use bold text and underlining in your notes to indicate where you need to do the oral equivalent of bold text to make your main points clear. That means changing your pace and volume, saying the words again, saying the idea again with different words or pausing to let the words sink in.

One downside of using full notes is the temptation to *read* the message rather than *preach* it. You need to be able to communicate in a way that enables you to speak naturally and look at your hearers.

You might write out key phrases in full, but use a simple prompt to indicate a story or illustration which you then retell without notes. If you use notes rather than full text then, if you're new to preaching, also write it out in full at some point in your preparation. This will force you to think about how you word everything you say. You're preaching God's word so you want to ensure that what you say is accurate, clear and powerful.

Number your pages just in case you drop your notes as you walk to the lectern, or get a loose-leaf folder to put your notes in.

Practise the talk. Ensure that your talk works as oral communication. Change phrases you stumble over. Check how long it is. Both of us preach our sermons aloud to our computers several times, making changes as we go along!

Keep referring back to your passage

It's important for people to see how what you're saying arises from your passage. If you do nothing else during the message, rub their noses in the Bible! You want people to see that you're not saying anything from the passage that they couldn't have got out of it for themselves. You're not only proclaiming the word of God to them, you are also teaching them to be self-feeders on the word. So don't point people to a passage while you continue to speak. Give them time to find the text and then read it aloud so everyone has read it.

Write out cross-references in full in your notes, but join the congregation in finding references in the Bible as you go.

Responding to the response

As you preach, there will be a response. As preachers we need to pick up on the sometimes subtle signs and respond to them, rather than just ploughing ahead with our next point.

- If you sense people are not grasping what you say, slow down and have another go.
- Congregations often go quiet when people are being convicted or when the truth is taking hold of their hearts. Don't rush on from this pliable moment. Press the truth home.
- On some occasions it might be worth stopping to pray, to worship, to invite the congregation to respond in adoration or confession as a result of what God is revealing. Don't be so tied to your preparation that you can't depart from it when need arises.

Finishing

You also need to think carefully about how you will end the sermon—not just what will be in the conclusion, but how you will transition to the next thing in the meeting. Hopefully by this point God has spoken to people through your words. You don't want to distract from this with confusion. Are you going to close in prayer? Are you handing over to someone else? Are you going to move straight to a song? Who's going to introduce it? Try to ensure, if you can, that what happens after the sermon reinforces its message or gives people an opportunity to respond.

Questions for reflection

Martyn Lloyd-Jones said preachers should preach with their whole personality, and with authority, freedom, seriousness, liveliness, zeal, warmth, urgency, persuasiveness, pathos or emotion, and power.[1]

- Which of those are your strongest qualities and which are your weakest? How do you shape your preaching to take advantage of these gifts? How can you develop your weak areas?

Lloyd-Jones also said: "The preacher while speaking should, in a sense, be deriving something from his congregation. There are those present in the congregation who are spiritually-minded people, and filled with the Spirit, and they make their contribution to the occasion. There is always an element of exchange in true preaching ... There is an interplay, action and response, and this often makes a very vital difference."[2]

- What's your experience of this interplay between preacher and congregation?

1 D. Martyn Lloyd-Jones, *Preaching and Preachers*, Zondervan, 2011, p 95-108.

2 D. Martyn Lloyd-Jones, *Preaching and Preachers*, Zondervan, 2011, p 98.

Ideas for action: Form a preachers' club

A "preachers' club" is a group of preachers who meet regularly for mutual support and development. Typically when you meet, you might review a sermon or present work in progress for constructive feedback.

Feedback

Ask one or two people you trust to give you feedback. If you're part of a preachers' club, then offer one another feedback. Be gentle—we want to improve our preaching without crushing one another. But offer genuine critique so people know how they can improve. And remember that feedback is not just pointing out problems—ensure you also highlight the strengths of the sermon. A good model is to highlight three things that went well for every one thing that could be improved.

Review questions

- Did the sermon capture the affections for Christ so lives would be changed? Did the sermon preach the glory of God for the glory of God?
- Was the main aim of the sermon clear? What was it? Did everything contribute to that aim?
- Did the sermon make the passage clear? Was the passage properly understood? Did the main points of the sermon reflect the content of the passage?
- Was the passage set in its immediate context? Was it set in the context of the Bible story as a whole? Did the sermon point to Christ?
- Did the sermon make the passage real? Was it clear how we should respond? Was the application relevant to the hearers?

- Did the sermon make the passage felt? Were gospel motives given for the application? Did the sermon sound like good news?
- Could the sermon be understood by everyone? Did it hold people's attention? Was it preached with genuine passion and conviction?
- Did the introduction make people want to keep listening? Did the sermon come to a fitting conclusion? Were illustrations used effectively?
- What were the sermon's best features? How could the sermon have been improved?

Caution

Identifying areas for improvement is crucial to growth. But there's an ever-present danger that we start listening to sermons with a critical spirit, becoming too highly attuned to their short-comings. The result is we end up sitting in judgment on the preacher rather than sitting under God's word.

Responding

The key is to approach any Bible message praying that we will hear God, and asking God to bless the preaching of his word. It will also help to ask the following questions:

- Has this person got it right and I've got it wrong?
- Even if they haven't got everything right, what are they saying that I need to hear?
- What is God actually saying in this passage?
- How can I encourage and help this preacher?
- How is God speaking to me through this preaching (despite its imperfections)?

16 PREPARING A BIBLE STUDY

Principle

Help people discover the message of the text by asking good questions.

Consider this

"I don't really like that interpretation."
"This is what it means for me."
"Everyone's entitled to their opinion."
"This is what I learned when I went through something similar."

Everyone seemed to be having a great time. They all had their Bibles open and were engaging with the text. But Phil felt uneasy. Was God's voice being heard? Or were people just hearing echoes of their own opinions?

Bible background

Read 1 Peter 1 v 22 – 2 v 3.

- How does Peter describe people and their opinions?
- How does Peter describe the word of God?
- What does the word of God do?

Read all about it

Bible studies have a number of strengths:

- They engage people in the learning process.
- They allow the Bible to be applied directly to the specifics of people's lives.
- People tend to learn better if learning directly applies to their lives and builds on what they already know.
- They allow a group to pray for each other and help each other live out what the Bible teaches.
- They allow for a degree of personal accountability. Perhaps it's not surprising that Jesus often taught by asking questions.

But interactive Bible studies also have some significant dangers:

- People can share stories rather than engaging with the text of Scripture.
- Every perspective can be treated as equally valid, so the voice of God in the Bible is not heard.

If everyone simply shares their own experiences, then you might have a good discussion, but you won't get to the point the Bible is teaching. Our experiences will be king and the Bible demoted so it becomes merely an echo of our experience. If, in contrast, the leader simply tells everyone what the Bible says, then you quickly get to the point, but there's little involvement and therefore little learning.

So what we're after in a good Bible study is everyone discovering together what the Bible says so there's good discussion *and* you get to the point the Bible is teaching. And that requires good preparation and a good leader. It's not something that can be done off the cuff any more than delivering a sermon.

Much of what we have said about sermons is also true of Bible studies. Their aim is just the same: **to capture the affections of our hearts for Christ so that lives are changed so that God is glorified.**

They, too, depend for their effectiveness on trust in the authority of the Bible and the power of the Spirit. They, too, should be focused on the gospel and point to Christ.

As with a sermon, the first step in Bible-study preparation is to identify a "main aim". The Bible is not open to *any* interpretation. It's much easier, however, for people to query the Bible's authority over them in a small-group setting than it is in the larger meeting. One consequence is that leaders need to have a firm doctrine of Scripture and the courage to correct gently when experience is elevated above the authority of the Bible.

The key to a good Bible study is to identify the main idea the Bible passage teaches, and the impact you want to have in the hearts and lives of your group. The *goal* of your Bible study is for people to grasp the message of the passage for themselves and the *means* is asking good questions.

There are many different approaches and it's good to use variety. You could invite people to share their stories on a theme and then explore how the word of God informs and transforms our experience. You can give a short monologue followed by a provocative application question.

The following is a good basic framework for putting interactive Bible studies together:

1. Introduction question
2. Investigation questions
3. Interpretation questions
4. Implication questions

This should be prefaced and concluded with prayer:

- submitting to God in prayer at the beginning and asking for help with understanding
- submitting to God in prayer at the end and asking for help with the implications

Introduction question

This should be like a good sermon introduction. After this question people should be thinking: "I'm glad I came this evening because this is going to be relevant to me". It helps if there are no wrong answers to this question ("How do you feel about...?" "Have you ever...?") as this helps get everyone contributing.

Investigation and interpretation questions

Investigation questions are designed to familiarise people with the passage. They are often "What?" questions. Interpretation questions get people to see why and how the passage says what it says. Investigation and interpretation questions should:

- get people into the passage or story.
- move people towards your main aim.

It can also be helpful to include a summary question. The answer to this question should be something like your main aim. Don't rush the study along to this point. If some bright spark gets it early on, ignore them. Let as many people as possible think their way to the message of the passage. This may be a good point for a monologue summary.

Implication questions

The aim is to relate the truth of the Bible to experience. So at this point you can allow people to discuss their experience more. You could ask people to identify one or two action points for themselves and the group. You can also make prayer part of the response.

Preparing good questions

Good Questions	Bad Questions
are clear	are too easy or dull
make people look at the passage	give the answer in the question
open up discussion	ask two questions in one
move people towards your aim	encourage speculation that takes people away from the text of Scripture
require some thought while not being too difficult	are too complicated

Open and closed questions

Closed questions have a limited range of answers ("What colour is the carpet?"). Open questions have a large or unlimited range of answers ("How do you feel about the colour of the carpet?") Open questions open up discussion. So don't ask an open question when you want a particular answer and don't ask a closed question when you want an open discussion. For example, instead of asking: "Does this story show us Jesus is King?" ask: "What does this story show us about Jesus?" A series of quick closed questions can be useful for summing up.

Here's a sample of possible questions:

- What do you find striking in the passage or story?
- How do you think the first readers or the people involved in the story felt?
- How would you have reacted?
- What do we learn about God in this passage or story?
- What do we learn about human beings in this passage or story?
- Where have we seen this in the Bible story before?
- What in this passage points to Jesus or shows our need for Jesus?
- What are the links to our lives?
- When have you faced a similar challenge?

- How are we like the people in the passage or story?
- How does the passage challenge or encourage you?
- How does the passage help us see what it means to walk in God's ways?
- When might you talk about this passage with a Christian?
- When might you talk about this passage with an unbeliever?

The key to writing good questions is to ask yourself how people might answer your questions cold (that is, without all the preparation you've been doing).

Here are some other approaches you may find helpful.

Case studies

You can encourage people to think through the implications of a passage by constructing case studies. Describe a situation or a person and then ask: "What would you do?" or "What would you say?" You could present the case study or studies at the beginning of your study time and then return to them after having looked at the passage.

Corporate meditation

Ask people to pray through the passage together. Read a verse or two at a time and ask people to respond with praise, thanksgiving, confession or supplication as appropriate. Then read out the next verse or two. The result will be a kind of "corporate meditation" on the passage. This works well for psalms and epistles.

Opposites

Considering the opposite of the truth which a passage teaches often helps to clarify the implications of what the passage actually does teach as well as what it opposes.

- Ask: "If someone *didn't* believe this, how would they behave?" People may begin to describe behaviours or emotions that they themselves currently exhibit.
- Ask people to write an opposite version of the passage. Again,

in doing so they may describe behaviours or emotions that they exhibit.

- Rewrite the passage (or part of the passage) in an opposite form and ask the group to "translate" back into its proper form.

Questions for reflection

- Take a passage that you are teaching soon and create a Bible study using the framework above with:
    - introduction question
    - investigation questions
    - interpretation questions
    - implication questions

- Review your questions in the light of the criteria above. How do they measure up?

Ideas for action

Following up a sermon

Many churches encourage small groups not to do a new Bible study, but to follow up the Sunday sermon. The primary focus is on exploring the implications of what has already been taught. In a small group we can push application into the specifics of our lives in a way that can't be done with a larger congregation. Try to focus this on implications that are specifically relevant to your group, even if this means you don't cover all the ideas in the sermon.

Here's a framework for doing this. It's based on two simple headings that are easy to remember:

1. **Engaging** with the message with our heads, hands and hearts, and
2. **Applying** the message in a personal, communal and missional way.

This is just a framework. It's best if you can tailor the questions and their order to the passage and the needs of your gospel community.

<table>
<tr><td>Intro</td><td colspan="2">1. How has the Spirit spoken to you through this section of God's word?</td></tr>
<tr><td>Head</td><td colspan="2">2. Do you have any questions? or How would you summarise the message of this section or story?</td></tr>
<tr><td rowspan="3">Hands</td><td>Personal</td><td>3. What are the implications for you?
or How does this section speak to your heart or life?</td></tr>
<tr><td>Communal</td><td>4. What are the implications for our group or church? or When might you talk about this section with a Christian?</td></tr>
<tr><td>Missional</td><td>5. What are the implications for those we want to reach? or When might you talk about this section with an unbeliever?</td></tr>
<tr><td>Heart</td><td colspan="2">6. What gospel motives does this section give?
or How should this section shape our love, hope, fears or desires?</td></tr>
</table>

17 LEADING A BIBLE STUDY

Principle

Keep people focused on the message of the text and its implications.

Consider this

"Peter knows so many Bible verses, doesn't he?" said Jenny. "Hmm," said Bob.

"I could never have made that connection to Ezekiel," Jenny continued. "Nor me," said Bob.

"And that stuff about eschatology was amazing. Way over my head." Bob said nothing.

"He seems to have something to say about everything," said Jenny. "Except the passage we're supposed to be studying," said Bob, this time to himself.

"He really knows his Bible."

"Then why are our Bible studies always better when he's away?" thought Bob.

Bible background
Read Ephesians 4 v 11-32

- Why did God give the church teachers and pastors (v 11-12)?
- How do we become mature (v 13-16)?
- How are we changed (v 17-24)?
- How are we to speak to one another (v 16, 25, 29)?

Read all about it

The key to leading productive Bible studies is to:

- keep people interacting with the Bible.
- keep the discussion moving towards your aim.

Start by asking a good reader to read the passage aloud. Don't ask people to read a verse each. This doesn't help understanding because it breaks up the flow of the passage. And pray. We need the Spirit of God to help us understand and apply the Bible.

Move the discussion towards your aim using supplementary questions:

- What do you mean by that?
- Why do you think that?
- What does everyone else think?
- How does this verse fit in?
- Where does it say that?
- What are the implications of that?

Don't be afraid of silences. People need time to think. And don't avoid conflict. It's often a sign that the Bible is challenging people's thinking and affections.

Keep an eye on time and keep things going. Don't let discussion go round in circles. Edit your material and activities as you go along. Leave time for prayer.

Think about who's speaking and who's not speaking. Try to reduce dominant voices and include quiet people. You could ask an assistant to monitor group dynamics and bring in uninvolved people.

You may find it helpful to split your group into smaller groups to discuss specific questions. This will encourage contributions from those who are reluctant to speak in a larger group. Giving groups a piece of flipchart paper helps focus discussion and feedback. If groups have been doing the same exercise, don't take feedback group by group as this usually involves repetition.

Finally, be prepared to learn yourself. Recognise that your understanding of the passage might be wrong.

Coping with wrong answers

- **Ask a question back**—either to the individual or to the group. ("Is that right?" "What do others think?" "What about verse 20?")
- **Pick out what is right in the answer and then point people to the correct point.** ("You're right to recognise that danger, but what does this passage say?")
- **Give scenarios which test the answer.** ("What that be a helpful thing to say to a new Christian?")
- **Ignore the answer,** hoping they will grasp the point as the Bible study unfolds.

Coping with difficult questions

- **Ask a question back**—either to the individual or to the group. ("What do you think?" "What do others think?")
- **Never be afraid to admit you don't know.** ("I'm not sure, but this is what I do know.")

Coping with irrelevant questions or digressions

- **Acknowledge the question or comment and then bring the discussion back.** ("That's an interesting issue, but the point here is this." "I'm not sure, but what I do knows this.")
- **A digression can sometimes lead to a fruitful discussion.** It might provide the opportunity for important learning even if that learning is unrelated to the passage in question.

More than a Bible study

Encourage your group to think of themselves not simply as an event (a Bible study), but a community of people supporting one another and doing mission together. Encourage them to spend time with each other outside the Bible study and to use this time to speak the truth in love to one another. And think about how you can serve in your church, reach your friends and bless your neighbourhood.

Ideas for action

Coping with difficult people

Silent Simon
May be unsure of himself, bored or intimidated. Respond positively to any contribution he makes—even if it's not a good one. Directly ask him a question or ask if he understands. If he's bored, invite people to contribute from their experience.

Dominant Dave
May just love the sound of his own voice or he may be over-enthusiastic. Take him aside and remind him of his responsibility to help others grow. Sit next to him to reduce eye contact—eye contact encourages contributions. Ask for contributions from those who've not yet spoken.

Tangential Tom
Often introduces red herrings. Ignore or acknowledge his comments, but then come back to the passage ("That's an interesting question, but the issue here is this").

Joking Jeremy
Can help the group get along, but if he starts to subvert the learning, stop laughing at his jokes.

Moaning Maureen
Repeatedly uses the group for a good moan. Acknowledge her issues, but keep the group focused on the gospel. Don't let her transform the group into a therapy group. Talk to her one to one outside the group, focusing her attention on the gospel.

Argumentative Ahmed
Can helpfully stir up debate. Perhaps he won't settle for clichés, which provokes the group to go deeper. Don't get upset. Find merit in what he says and then move on. Ask the group what they think.

Know-it-all Norman
Wants to display his knowledge. Jump in and ask for group comment. Speak to him outside the group. Bring him in on your side to help the group grow.

Whispering Wilma
Conducts whispered conversations with her neighbour. Stop talking and let everyone listen. Ask if she has something to share with the group as a whole (without being sarcastic).

Summary

- Acknowledge comments and move on.
- Ask the group to comment on people's contributions.
- Remind people outside the meeting of their responsibility to the group.
- Use your body language and comments to encourage quiet people and discourage disruptive people.

SELECTED FURTHER READING

- John Chapman, *Setting Hearts on Fire: A Guide to Giving Evangelistic Talks*, Matthias Media.
- Tim Keller, *Preaching to the Heart,* audio lectures, www.gordon-conwellstore.or
- John Piper, *The Supremacy of God in Preaching*, Baker.
- John Stott, *Between Two Worlds: The Challenge of Preaching Today*, Eerdmans; or *I Believe in Preaching*, Hodder & Stoughton.
- Colin Marshall, *Growth Groups Manual*, Matthias Media.
- Gilbert Lennox, *Getting the Message: A Hands-On Guide to Personal Bible Study*, Cedar Hill Trust.

Other titles by Tim Chester

Work Songs

Exploring frustration, compromise, stress and joy from the Psalms

Six studies looking at six psalms to "sing" in the workplace. For many Christians there is a gap between church on Sunday and work on Monday. These songs encourage us to bridge that gap. Great for workers everywhere and ideal for working through in twos or threes as well as in larger groups.

Living in the real world

The Good Book Guide to 1 Peter

Wise Christians understand that opposition and suffering are normal for the church and are prepared for anything. That's why Christians today need the message of 1 Peter—a letter to first-century believers surrounded by trials and hostility. Why does God let this happen? How can my faith survive? How should I treat those who cause me suffering? These questions and more are covered in five sessions full of practical application. Let's be prepared, so that our faith "may be proved genuine and may result in praise, glory and honour when Jesus Christ is revealed".

FOR MORE INFORMATION AND TO ORDER:
UK and Europe: www.thegoodbook.co.uk
North America: www.thegoodbook.com
Australia: www.thegoodbook.com.au
New Zealand: www.thegoodbook.co.nz

Gospel centred leadership

becoming the leader God wants you to be

Our world is awash with leadership trainers and gurus, claiming to show how people can do their job better. But Christians only have one role model for leadership in practice—the Lord Jesus Christ. And the leadership he calls us to is radically different to the kind of leadership the world looks to. It is humble and servant hearted. Use this book to grow into the servant-hearted leader that God wants you to be.

By Steve Timmis

Gospel centred work

becoming the worker God wants you to be

In *Gospel-centred work* you'll discover how the good news about Jesus transforms the way we think about our work in surprising and practical ways. Use this book on your own or with a group of colleagues to discover how we serve a working God; how Christian belief transforms the central problems we experience with work; and how the workplace can be a place for long-term effective gospel witness.

By Tim Chester

FOR MORE INFORMATION AND TO ORDER:
UK and Europe: www.thegoodbook.co.uk
North America: www.thegoodbook.com
Australia: www.thegoodbook.com.au
New Zealand: www.thegoodbook.co.nz

Gospel centred church

becoming the community God wants you to be

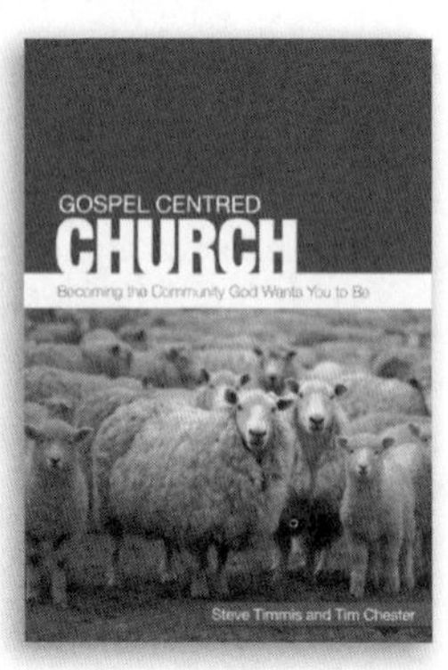

In *Gospel-centred church*, Steve Timmis and Tim Chester explain that gospel ministry is much more than simply evangelism. It is about shaping the whole of our church life and activities by the content and imperatives of the gospel. It is about ensuring that our church or group is motivated by and focused on the gospel, as opposed to our traditions. This workbook is designed to help clarify our thinking about how we should live our lives as the people of God.

Gospel centred life

becoming the person God wants you to be

How can ordinary Christians live the truly extraordinary life that God calls us to? By focusing our attention on the grace of God shown to us in the gospel, everyday problems, familiar to Christians everywhere, can be transformed as the cross of Christ becomes the motive and measure of everything we do. *Gospel-centred life* shows how every Christian can follow the way of the cross as they embrace the liberating grace of God.

FOR MORE INFORMATION AND TO ORDER:
UK and Europe: www.thegoodbook.co.uk
North America: www.thegoodbook.com
Australia: www.thegoodbook.com.au
New Zealand: www.thegoodbook.co.nz

Gospel centred marriage

becoming the couple God wants you to be

To understand why marriages struggle—as they all do—we need to understand the nature of our sin. To make marriages work, we need to understand how to apply the truth about God and his salvation. This study guide on Christian marriage focuses on how the gospel shapes the practical realities of everyday life. Tim Chester lifts the lid on many of the common pressure points, and shows how a proper understanding of the gospel can shape a response.

Gospel centred family

becoming the parents God wants you to be

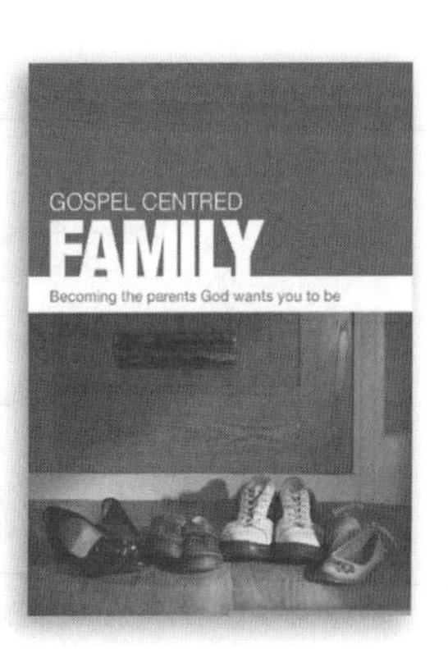

Many books aim to raise up competent, balanced parents and well-trained, well-rounded children. But Tim Chester and Ed Moll focus on families growing God-knowing, Christ-confessing, grace-receiving, servant-hearted, mission-minded believers—adults and children together. In twelve concise chapters, this book challenges us to become the distinctively different people that God, through his gospel, calls us to be.

FOR MORE INFORMATION AND TO ORDER:
UK and Europe: www.thegoodbook.co.uk
North America: www.thegoodbook.com
Australia: www.thegoodbook.com.au
New Zealand: www.thegoodbook.co.nz